A Trackless Path

Books and Translations by Ken McLeod

    A Trackless Path (2016)

    Reflections on Silver River (2014)

    An Arrow to the Heart (2007)

    Wake Up to Your Life (2001)

    The Great Path of Awakening (1987)

A Trackless Path

A commentary on the great completion (dzogchen) teaching of
Jigmé Lingpa's *Revelations of Ever-present Good*

Ken McLeod

Unfettered Mind Media
Pragmatic Buddhism
Sonoma, California

Copyright © 2016 Ken McLeod

All rights reserved under International and Pan-American Copyright Conventions. No part of this book may be used or reproduced in any manner whatsoever without written permission from the publisher, except in the case of brief quotations embodied in critical articles and reviews.

McLeod, Ken., 1948–
A trackless path: a commentary on the great completion (dzogchen) teaching of Jigmé Lingpa's Revelations of Ever-present Good / Ken McLeod. — First edition. — Sonoma CA: Unfettered Mind Media, [2016]
pages ; cm.
ISBN: 978-0-9895153-4-4
Includes bibliographical references.
1. Buddhism. 2. Rdzogs-chen. 3. Religion.
4. Religion — Comparative studies. 5. Spiritual life — Buddhism. 6. Religious life — Buddhism.
7. Philosophy. 8. Contemplation. 9. Meditation.
I. 'Jigs-med-gling-pa Rang-byung-rdo-rje, 1729 or 1730–1798. Revelations of ever-present good.
II. Title.
BQ4302 .M448 2016
294.3/444 — dc23

1512

Unfettered Mind Media
www.unfetteredmind.org

Printed in the United States of America
Cover photo: Diana Chang
Book design: VJB/Scribe

9 8 7 6 5 4 3 2

Go where there is no path
and leave no trail

For Kilung Rinpoche

Contents

Introduction   3
Revelations of Ever-present Good   15

Commentary   27
    Eight conceptual approaches   29
    Timeless freedom in great completion   61
    Elimination of errors   89

Acknowledgments   125
Bibliography   127
About the Author   129

A Trackless Path

Introduction

In 2003, I participated in a three-week retreat at Tara Mandala led by Dza Kilung Rinpoche. I went to the retreat with more than a little trepidation. Ever since I had left the three-year retreat center at Kagyu Ling in France in 1983, quite serious problems in mind and body would arise whenever I engaged in even moderately intensive practice.

Tsultrim Allione had invited me to the retreat and kindly lodged me in a lovely little cabin where I was on my own and could take care of myself. The cabin had a magnificent view overlooking the hills of southern Colorado. From the small balcony I could watch the sky, the play of clouds and the lightning that often flashed in the distance, and pursue meditation and practice as much as body and mind permitted. The walks up and down the hill, from the dining area to the teaching hall, provided me with plenty of exercise to counteract the tendency for energy to stagnate in my system. Kilung Rinpoche taught each morning from Longchenpa's *Chö-ying Dzö* (Tib. *chos-dbyings rin-po-che'i mdzod*). For meditation instruction, he simply said to do nothing and left the rest up to us.

A bit to my surprise and much to my relief, my fears of recurrent problems were never realized. In this environment I was able to practice consistently without becoming ill — for the first time in twenty years. That retreat started a process of unfolding experience that continues to this day.

At the end of the retreat, Kilung Rinpoche showed me a short text by the eighteenth-century Tibetan mystic Jigmé Lingpa. The way he unwrapped the text and gave it to me told me more than words ever could that this text was dear to his heart. He said that he would be grateful if I could translate it into English. The text was a poem about the practice of *dzogchen* (great completion) and effectively summarized all that we had studied during the retreat. It was a bit difficult to understand in places, due largely to Jigmé Lingpa's style of writing, but with Gerardo Abboud's help, I translated it and presented the translation to Rinpoche. A few years later, I taught the text at a retreat in

New Mexico. Now, encouraged by the response to my recent book *Reflections on Silver River*, I have retranslated that poem and written this commentary.

Over fifty years ago, D. T. Suzuki's *Essays in Zen Buddhism* struck a chord in me. They awoke a feeling and a yearning that I could not put into words. The reverberations of that chord led me to abandon a career in mathematics and journey to India where I met my principal teacher Kalu Rinpoche. The reverberations did not stop there. Later, Thomas Merton's *The Wisdom of the Desert*, a compendium of anecdotes and sayings from the early Christian anchorites in the Egyptian deserts, set off reverberations with another chord. The common theme was a resonance with a certain kind of awareness — a knowing that was vitally important to me, more important than what I did with my life.

Why did I and why do I pursue that knowing? In the end, it is simply because this knowing calls to me. In traditional Buddhism, this knowing is presented as nirvana, enlightenment, freedom, awakening, the end of suffering or any number of other promises. For me, those words now ring hollow. I think I believed them at one point, but I am not sure. The call of that knowing, however, has never been in doubt, and it still calls.

Spiritual Practice and Artistic Expression: An Analogy

While spiritual practice is not simply or even principally an aesthetic interest, I have found the analogy of artistic expression helpful in understanding the path I have taken, whether the expression is through painting, music or dance. When a musician learns to play an instrument or even a single piece of music, he or she begins a journey. No one knows or can know where that journey will lead. Maybe a teacher or a respected friend or colleague suggested that particular piece. Maybe the musician heard someone else play it and it moved something inside. What is important here is that he or she feels a call and is moved to respond. Whereas the call of music is usually to an aesthetic experience, the call of spiritual practice is to a different relationship with life itself. For me that calling took the form of a knowing, a knowing that was evident in the accounts of Buddhist masters, Christian mystics and, later, Sufi and Taoist sages.

Both art and spiritual practice have their own practice regimens. Art often involves long periods of rigorous training. Sometimes the training is even harsh, as in ballet and other forms of dance. Art also involves a kind of asceticism that is often similar to renunciation, a relationship with a teacher that may be hard to understand from a conventional perspective and a call to an ideal that is difficult, if not impossible, to put into words. From a utilitarian perspective, neither art nor spiritual practice produces something that is useful in the world. In fact, a use or the lack thereof is one of the criteria that Canadian customs officials use to determine whether an item is to be considered art. Today, there are innumerable explorations of the application of spiritual methods to conventional life (training in mindfulness, for example), and much research on the evolutionary origins of compassion and altruism, all with a view to helping us improve our lives and possibly improve the functioning of society. I have never felt that the purpose of either art or spiritual practice is to improve our lives in the conventional sense, or to make us healthier, better people or to help us be more successful, however one wants to define that pernicious notion.

Another analogy between art and spiritual practice is the matter of talent. I do not have much musical talent, but I once learned to play a couple of instruments passably. Even that took a lot of practice. I could not comprehend how some people could just pick up an instrument and play it — and play it well. Equally amazing to me were those who could listen to a piece of music and not only play it but embellish or improvise from it. The same holds true in spiritual practice. Some people have to work long and hard just to be able to meditate at all. Other people seem to be able to meditate very easily. Still others seem to have a natural relationship with the subtle awareness that is the focus of many Buddhist practices. Understanding comes to them quickly. Nevertheless, people with natural talent do not necessarily have an easier time. They often have to work long and hard, too, both to realize the potential of their talent and to work through the difficulties and challenges it presents to them. Einstein, for instance, once wrote to a young girl, "Do not worry about your difficulties in mathematics. I can assure you mine are still greater."

Not infrequently, when a musician is mastering an instrument, that pursuit leads to unexpected difficulties. Similarly, the pursuit of the knowing that called to me led to difficulties that I could never have imagined. The challenges I faced over the years forced me to examine again and again what was I doing and why. Those re-examinations ruthlessly stripped away the ornate prose, the rich poetry, and the glowing accounts that abound in traditional texts.

All that remained was a profound simplicity that I saw running through all the sutras, the tantras, the commentaries and all the different methods of practice that have evolved over the centuries. This simplicity illuminates from within, making all the sutras and other writings transparent and clear. It is the genesis of the traditions and forms of practice that evolved in different countries and different cultures, and of the texts, rituals, ceremonies, worldviews, beliefs and other repositories of trust and faith. It is also what all those cultural artifacts are about. They both come from and point to this simplicity.

When we read poems such as Jigmé Lingpa's, possibilities open—possibilities we may never have thought of or possibilities we may have sensed but did not know how to pursue. Practice is about exploring those possibilities, and we do so because they are or become intensely meaningful to us. At some point, we may also feel compelled to give them expression and put them before others, too.

Awareness

The subject matter of this poem is a particular kind of awareness, an awareness that cannot be described. It can only be experienced. The practice regimen associated with it is called *dzogchen* or *great completion*.

In every contemplative tradition that I know, mention is made of a point where what is experienced cannot be put into words. The conceptual mind has reached its limits. *The Cloud of Unknowing* is the title of a book by a fourteenth-century mystic, in which the reader is counseled to seek God through contemplation that is motivated by love and stripped of all thought. In Mahayana Buddhism, the perfection of wisdom is described as inexpressible, indescribable and inconceivable. In this poem, too, Jigmé Lingpa states in the first verse that awareness cannot be described.

This book is about an awareness that goes beyond the conceptual mind. As such, it speaks to practitioners of many contemplative traditions, from Zen to Sufism, from Lao Tzu to Meister Eckhart. If you think this awareness will make you a better person or improve your life, then I suggest you close this book now and throw it away. Neither this poem nor this awareness has much to do with the utilitarian mentality that seems to pervade modern life, a mentality that, as David Graeber argues in *Debt: The First 5000 Years*, sees every human interaction as nothing more than a transaction, every kind act as a loan and every moral transgression as a debt to be repaid.

Whether this awareness is described as an awakening or as a deep peace, it opens up a profound freedom. It changes our relationship with what we experience, and it changes our relationship with life. Yet, if we look past the elaborate metaphors, the enigmatic stories and the naïve fables, we see from the lives of teachers and masters through the ages that this knowing does not necessarily make life easier. In more than a few cases, it made life considerably harder. Buddha Shakyamuni died largely abandoned by his followers. Milarepa, the great Tibetan mountain hermit renowned for his teaching songs, was assassinated by an envious scholar. Taranatha, one of the greatest scholar-masters of the Tibetan traditions, was implicated in a political plot, his monasteries confiscated and his writings proscribed for centuries. Nevertheless, few who seek this knowing have any regrets about their decision to pursue it. The knowing is meaningful, intensely meaningful, to them on its own.

Jigmé Lingpa and Great Completion

Jigmé Lingpa was a natural mystic. He lived as a mountain hermit, spending most of his life in one retreat setting or another. He practiced in the Nyingma (Tib. *rnying ma*) tradition, *The Ancient Ones*. It is the earliest of the Tibetan traditions of Buddhism and traces its beginning in Tibet to the eighth century and in India back to the first century CE. Jigmé Lingpa was regarded as an incarnation of the great fourteenth-century teacher Longchenpa, who in his *Seven Treasuries* organized the Nyingma teachings into a coherent body of practice. Though largely self-taught, Jigmé Lingpa was a prolific writer as well as a revealer of hidden teachings (Tib. *gter ma*, pron. *terma*). His most important revealed teaching is the *Heart Drop Cycle* (Tib. *klong chen snying thig*, pron. *long-chen nying-tik*), more or less the backbone of the Nyingma tradition today.

This poem, indeed the whole *Heart Drop Cycle,* is regarded as a mind treasure (Tib. *dgongs gter,* pron. *gongter*), that is, a text or a series of texts that arises spontaneously in the mind of the treasure-revealer. It is attributed not to Jigmé Lingpa but directly to Ever-present Good (Skt. *Samantabhadra*, Tib. *kun-tu bzang-po*). Ever-present Good is the embodiment of the buddha principle in the Nyingma tradition. The good referred to in his name is a good beyond the dualistic framework of good and evil. This good is a quality that is held to be present in every moment of experience. Ever-present Good thus represents both the potential for awakening and the expression of full awakening. As in many revealed teachings, this poem is presented as the spoken teaching of Ever-present Good. This mode of presentation expresses one of the underlying themes of dzogchen practice: full awakening is already present and nothing new needs to be created or developed — a practice of no practice.

In the spiritual domain, the matter of talent may be partially responsible for a long-standing debate in the Chan tradition of Chinese Buddhism, the debate between sudden awakening and gradual awakening. This debate was played out in Tibet at the end of the ninth century. A Chinese teacher named Mahayana visited Tibet and taught a form of practice based on sudden awakening, a practice of no practice in which awakening is held to be naturally present and just needs to be recognized. This approach was in direct contrast to the path of practice taught in Tibet up to that time, the sequential development of the various qualities that make awakening possible. Kamalashila, a former professor at Nalanda, the great Buddhist university in India, was invited to come to Tibet to debate with Mahayana and defend the view of gradual awakening or awakening in stages. Over a two-year period, Kamalashila and the Chinese monk debated their respective approaches at Samyé, the oldest Buddhist monastery in Tibet. The debate itself was inconclusive: neither side could comprehend the other. Nevertheless, the king of Tibet declared Kamalashila the winner and banned the teaching of sudden awakening in Tibet.

As a consequence, even into the twentieth century, any teaching in Tibet of a practice of no practice ran the risk of being attacked by orthodox scholars and practitioners as advocating the discredited approach of sudden awakening, particularly if it did not have a clear line of transmission back to Indian origins. Revealed texts such as this one, while deeply respected and valued in the Nyingma and other traditions, were often called into question, if not proscribed, by adherents to Tibetan orthodoxy.

The debate between sudden awakening and gradual awakening is, in some respects, similar to the debate between self-power and other-power in the Japanese traditions and between self-emptiness and other-emptiness in the Tibetan tradition. For some people, awakening seems to just happen. For others, it seems to be the end result of a developmental progression. For some people, awakening seems to come through their own efforts. For others, it feels as if it comes from outside. For some practitioners, all experience, even the experience of awakening, is groundless, empty. For others, something has definitely happened, and all that came before now seems utterly empty. My own teacher, despite my best efforts, consistently refused to engage these issues. When I pressed him on any of these matters, he would only say, "When you understand, you see they are not different." There is a great mystery here, no doubt, but I think it is the mystery of human experience and little is to be gained by trying to resolve these differences one way or the other.

In writing this book, I have drawn on my own training, which, largely because of Kalu Rinpoche's guidance, has always been a combination of working with practices from both the path of method (Tib. *thabs lam*, pron. *tab lam*) and the path of release (Tib. *grol lam*, pron. *drol lam*). The former consists of working with such meditations as death and impermanence, compassion or deity practice, all of which methodically build various capabilities. The latter is more about letting things unfold on their own, as in mahamudra or dzogchen practice. Jigmé Lingpa was a person of extraordinary spiritual talent, yet the *Heart Drop Cycle*, the major collection of his revealed texts, includes practices from both the path of method and the path of release. Sometimes, when what is arising for me is overwhelming, I find methodical-path practices give me something to work with and thus help me to stay in the experience and not fall into reaction. Other times, even when what is arising is so painful that I would not wish it on my worst enemy, I am able to rely on release-path practice and be completely clear and at peace in it. In the end, it is up to each of us to find the combination of practices that works for us and to make that our path.

Great Completion (Tib. *rdzogs chen*, pron. *dzogchen*) is a tradition of meditation practices based on the principle that a timeless awareness is present in every moment of experience, or, to put it another way, that every moment of experience is simultaneously a moment of timeless awareness and that every such moment is complete in and of itself. Following a teaching from Garab Dorje (Tib. *dga' rab rdo rje*), the Indian progenitor of the Great Completion tradition, the task of the practitioner is threefold: to recognize timeless awareness in each and every experience; to be in touch with that timeless awareness whatever he or she is experiencing; and to trust that all thinking or confusion resolves itself in that timeless awareness.

There are, broadly speaking, two approaches to great completion practice: *cutting through* (Tib. *khregs chod*, pron. *trekchö*) and *crossing over* (Tib. *thod rgal*, pron. *tögal*). In *cutting through*, the practitioner rests in attention and lets that attention cut through the confusion of thought and projection to the natural purity of timeless awareness itself. In *crossing over*, the practitioner directly enters a timeless awareness that is naturally present. These two approaches are complementary, and most practitioners engage both. This poem falls into the *cutting through* approach and emphasizes resting in the natural purity of mind itself.

The preceding description of great completion practice is analogous to the technical explanations that museums provide for a painting or sculpture on display or the program notes that describe a symphony. As such, it does little to communicate the experience of the mystery of awareness or how to practice. In his poem "Revelations of Ever-present Good," Jigmé Lingpa does both — he reveals the experience of timeless awareness directly from the experience itself, represented as Ever-present Good, and he describes what to do and not do to attune to this knowing.

Poems such as this one are intended for people for whom contemplative practice is a core element, if not *the* core element, of their lives. They are written for those who seek or sought direct experience rather than conceptual understanding. The teachings contained in these poems are poetic expressions of the kind of experiences that are highly valued by mystics and contemplatives. They are simultaneously a joyous celebration of those experiences and a method of communicating to others how to attune themselves to them. This book is intended for practitioners in any contemplative tradition who are drawn to a peace or freedom that can only be found when we touch a knowing that is free from the projections of thought and feeling.

On Translation

A poem such as this presents many challenges to a translator. Translation is often understood as a process of converting a text (whether a novel, a set of technical instructions or a poem) from one language to another. From this perspective, the greatest compliment one can bestow on a translation is that it is faithful to the original.

Such a view overlooks many factors that a translator must consider. Because the translator's knowledge and experience embrace another language and culture, he or she necessarily understands the text in a different way from those whose only language is the language of the original text. Likewise, the translator's understanding of the vocabulary and culture of the original is necessarily different from the author's or the poet's understanding. The readers of a translation are also quite different from the readers of the original text—they live in different times, different settings and different cultures. The language in which the translator writes has a different vocabulary, different associations and different methods of expression from those of the original language. Thus a translation is not a reproduction but a creative work in its own right and will necessarily differ from the original in substantial ways.

Traduttore, traditore the Italians say: translator, traitor. A translator is always suspect. He or she has access to knowledge that the other parties do not. One constantly has to ask, "Where do the translator's loyalties lie?" The uncertainty is particularly problematic in the case of a translator for an occupying army, whether the translator is from the army or from the conquered citizens. The same problem is present in the translation of Tibetan texts into English. For example, one of the Tibetan words for *mind* can be translated (and probably should be translated) as *heart* in many contexts. One translator might say, "Place your mind on the breath." Another translator might say, "Feel the breath with your heart." Both translators would feel that they were being faithful to the Tibetan, to the instruction and to their experience in practice, but most readers would see these two statements as two different instructions. This simple example illustrates why the notion of a faithful translation is quite misleading.

The translation of poems in particular requires a creative effort. The translator seeks to find a way to express in a different language what he or she understands and experiences in reading the poem in its original language. He or she does so with the intention that the reader experience something of what the translator felt and understood from the original poem. One might think of translation in this context as the process of taking a work of art in one medium and transforming it into another; for instance, taking a play by Shakespeare and composing an opera, as Verdi did with *Macbeth*. Another way to think about translation is that, for the reader in our culture, a text in Tibetan is a flower in bud. It is the translator's task to make the bud flower in the mind of the reader.

About This Book

Several years ago, a student sent me a card containing a quotation from Ralph Waldo Emerson: "Do not go where the path may lead, go instead where there is no path and leave a trail." The quotation struck me as an expression of the modern impetus to open new territory for others, but it did not ring true to me as far as spiritual practice was concerned. Many times I have had the feeling that practice is like venturing into the vast grasslands of the Canadian prairies, the Mongolian steppes or the Argentine pampas — a journey into a space that has no bound and retains no trace of one's passage. The image of a trackless path inspired the last two retreats I led, retreats in which I let go of the formal teacher role and acted only as an advisor to those attending while they explored their own paths of practice. A trackless path is for me a fitting image of the practice described in this book, a path of practice in which nothing is left of us, not even our footprints.

In writing this book, I have kept those retreats in mind, or, to be more precise, I have kept in mind those who came to those retreats. All were experienced practitioners, often with ten or more years of meditation behind them. They came from a variety of traditions and training but one trait they shared was that they knew they had reached the limits of conceptual knowing and wanted to go further. The starting point for this book is an acceptance that to know directly the mystery of awareness, the mystery of this experience we call life, we have to let the conceptual mind go.

Jigmé Lingpa composed this poem in three sections. The first section outlines a number of ways that conceptual thinking and conceptually based practices lead us to various kinds of dead ends. Here he is deliberately ironic, playfully pointing out the foibles and traps that we succumb to in spiritual practice. In the second section, he sets out his approach to great completion practice, using traditional frameworks to drive home the point that practice consists of letting go of the conceptual mind — utterly and completely. The third section points out common errors that practitioners make, subtle ways in which they allow the conceptual mind to reassert itself. In all of this, Jigmé Lingpa is not setting up the conceptual mind as an enemy to be defeated. Such an approach would entrench the propensity to relate to experience conceptually. Instead, he sees awakening as already present and the conceptual mind as a distorted way of experiencing life, a distortion that can be allowed to untie and release itself.

As for the commentary, from the day that Kilung Rinpoche gave me this text, Jigmé Lingpa's poem has moved me deeply. Here I have set out not what you should experience, nor even what you should do, but the ways I have found to attune to Jigmé Lingpa's words and where that has led me. I encourage you to read the book as you might read a poem, paying attention not so much to the meaning of the words but to what happens in you as you read them. To this end, I have sought to make both the translation and the commentary free from obstacles and distractions, using plain yet evocative English, avoiding technical vocabulary as much as possible and eschewing footnotes and other scholastic appendages.

If you are reading this book, you probably have a good bit of practice experience already. I suggest you read one or two verse commentaries at a time and see what resonates in you. Read them with a quiet, open mind. When you feel a shift, let it work inside you. Put the book down and rest right there, if only for a moment or two. When you sit down to practice, you may recall that shift. Do not think about what you have just read. That is just distraction. Do not try to go back to the shift or duplicate it. Simply rest in its echoes — in your body and your mind. In this way, these words may lead you into unknown territory, territory that is inaccessible to the conceptual mind. Where that may take you, what may become of you, I have no idea. I can, however, say this: no matter what the difficulties, no matter what the challenges, if you listen deeply to what calls to you in these pages and go where it leads you, I doubt very much that you will have any regrets.

གློང་ཆེན་སྙིང་གི་ཐིག་ལེ་ལས༈ ཀུན་ཏུ་བཟང་པོའི་དགོངས་ནམས་བཞུགས༈

དུས་པ་ཀུན་ཏུ་བཟང་པོ་ལ་ཕྱག་འཚལ་ལོ༈

རྩ་བ་ཆོད་པའི་སེམས་ཉིད་ནམ་མཁའ་འདུ༈
ནམ་མཁའི་རང་བཞིན་ནམ་མཁའ་དམིགས་སུ་མེད༈
དེ་བཞིན་རིག་པ་དཔེ་ཡིས་མི་མཚོན་ཡང་༈
ཐབས་ལ་བརྟེན་ནས་གཏན་གྱི་མན་ངག་བཤད༈
ཇི་ལྟར་དཔལ་པོའི་ཁྱིམ་གྱི་གཏེར་བཟང་པོ༈
རང་ལ་ཡོད་ཀྱང་དེ་ཉིད་མ་རིག་པས༈
དབུལ་པོའི་རང་བཞིན་འགྱུར་བ་མེད་པ་ལྟར༈
མ་རིག་རྟོག་པའི་དུ་བར་འཕྲུམས་ཆེས་པའི༈
མ་རྟོགས་འཁོར་བའི་སེམས་ཅན་སྙིང་རེ་རྗེ༈
ཇི་ལྟར་རྣལ་མའི་ལམ་ལ་རྒྱབ་ཕྱོགས་ནས༈
ལོག་པའི་འདུ་ཤེས་ཞིན་དུ་མི་བཟད་པས༈
རྟག་ཆད་ཁ་ན་མ་ཐོས་ཀུན་པའི་མཐའ༈
ཕྱོགས་གཅིག་ཁོར་འཛིན་པའི་དགའ་བུབ་ཅན༈
ལོག་རྟོག་སྨུ་སྟེགས་ཅན་དག་སྙིང་རེ་མོངས༈
གདོད་ནས་དག་པའི་སེམས་ཉིད་ནམ་མཁའི་ཁམས༈
ཤེས་བྱའི་ཆོས་ཀྱི་ཇི་ལྟར་བཙལ་བྱུས་ཀྱང་༈
སྲིད་བྱིའི་ཁ་རྒྱས་དེ་ཉིད་འཆིང་བ་ལྟར༈
དོན་ལ་རྒྱབ་ཀྱིས་ཕྱོགས་པའི་མདོ་ཞིན་ཅན༈
ནན་ཐོས་འགོག་པའི་བློ་ཅན་ཨ་ཐང་ཆད༈
འཁོར་འདས་ཀུན་གྱི་རྩ་བ་རང་གི་སེམས༈
བཅས་བཅོས་མེད་པའི་ངང་དུ་སངས་རྒྱས་པ༈
མ་རིག་རྟེན་འབྲེལ་འཁོར་བའི་ཆོས་འཁོར་ལ༈
འདུ་ཤེས་གཅིག་ཏུ་གཞུངས་པའི་ཕྱོགས་འཛིན་ཅན༈
རང་རྒྱལ་བཅོམ་མའི་སངས་རྒྱས་རྣམས་རེ་དགའད༈

Revelations of Ever-present Good

from the *Great Vastness Heart Drop Cycle*

I bow to the aware Ever-present Good.

Eight conceptual approaches

Once known, mind itself is like space.
The nature of space is that there is nothing that is space.
In the same way, examples cannot really point out awareness.
Yet I rely on such methods to shed light on key points.

What is it like when a poor man has
A priceless treasure in his home
But doesn't know it? Just as he remains poor,
You remain entangled in a net of unaware thinking—
How heartbreaking, you beings, benighted in samsara!

What is it like when you turn your back on the natural path?
Because you are enthralled by mistaken beliefs,
Your puritanical practice is lopsided,
Based as it is on some flawed metaphysical theory—
How reactive you are, you irrational extremists!

Mind itself, originally pure, is like space.
As long as you look for it with conceptual tools,
You are like a bug encasing itself in its own spit—
In your obsession, you turn your back on what is truly meaningful.
How worn out you must be, you listeners, from rejecting everything!

Mind is the source of all experience, patterned or free.
You wake up completely when you rest and do nothing at all.
Instead, you are dogmatic and single-minded in your belief
In the teachings of ignorance, interdependence and samsara.
How pleased you must be, you self-reliant ones, with your artificial awakening!

གདོད་ནས་རང་རྒྱལ་རྟོགས་པའི་སེམས་ཉིད་དེ༔
མ་བཅོས་གཤུག་མའི་ཀློམས་སུ་ཞུགས་པ་ལ༔
བདེན་གཉིས་ཆིག་ལ་འཆེལ་བའི་རྟོག་དཔྱོད་ཀྱིས༔
ཡིན་ཚུལ་བཅོས་མར་གདོང་བའི་ཚུལ་འཆོས་ཅན༔
བྱང་ཆུབ་སེམས་དཔའི་གྱུབ་མཐའ་ཕྱི་ཕྲག་རིང་༔
བཟང་ངན་བླང་དོར་མེད་པའི་སེམས་ཉིད་ལ༔
གཅོང་བཅོག་སྦྱོང་ལེན་སྐྱིན་པའི་ལྔད་ཀྱིས་བསླུད༔
གཉིས་མེད་དོན་ལ་གཉིས་འཛིན་གཟུགས་ཀྱིས་བཅོས༔
ཐོབ་བུ་མེད་ལ་གོ་འཕང་དོན་གཉེར་བའི༔
བུ་རྒྱུད་ཀྱི་ཡའི་གྱུབ་མཐའ་སྣམས་རེ་མཚར༔
བཟང་ངན་འཧེལ་འགྲིབ་མེད་པའི་གནས་ལུགས་ལ༔
ལྷ་སྣོམ་སྦྱོང་པའི་བ་སྤྱོད་འགག་ན་ཡང་༔
ཐབས་དང་ཤེས་རབ་སྦྱོང་པའི་དངོས་འཛིན་ནོས༔
བྱར་མེད་བུ་བར་གཡེལ་བའི་གྱུབ་མཐའ་ཅན༔
སྤྱོད་རྒྱུད་ཨུ་པའི་བརྒྱལ་ཞུགས་ཤང་རེ་ཆད༔
ཡི་ནང་བར་མཚམས་མེད་པ་དུན་པའི་གཤིས༔
བཅོས་མའི་བློ་དང་བྲལ་བའི་སེམས་ཉིད་ལ༔
ཟབ་གསལ་ཡུག་རྒྱུར་བཅོས་པའི་ནུས་རྟོག་ཅན༔
རྒྱལ་འབྱོར་ཡོ་གའི་གྱུབ་མཐའ་ཅོད་རེ་ཆུང་༔
འབད་རྩོལ་རྒྱལ་མ་ཙིས་སེམས་ཀྱི་དང་༔
འབྲས་བུ་ལམ་དུ་བྱེད་པའི་ཆོས་ཉིད་ལ༔
རྩ་རྒྱུང་སེམས་ཀྱི་ངལ་བསོས་དབུགས་འབྱིན་པའི༔
སྦྱོས་བཙུམ་ཨ་ནུའི་གྱུབ་མཐའ་ཐང་རེ་ཆད༔
ཞལ་ཕུག་མཚན་མ་བྲལ་བའི་སེམས་ཉིད་ལ༔
སྣང་སྲིད་ལྷ་སྐུར་ལྷ་བའི་གོལ་ས་དང་༔
སྦྲར་གྲགས་ཕྲགས་སུ་གོལ་བའི་འཛིན་རྟོག་ཅན༔
མ་དུ་ཡོ་གའི་ལམ་གྱིས་འདི་མི་མཐོང་༔
ཀུན་དུ་བཟང་པོའི་དགོངས་སྣམས་ལས༔
ཡིག་བརྒྱུད་བློ་ཡི་གྱུབ་མཐའ་གཟག་པའི་ལེའུ་སྟེ་དང་པོའི༔

Mind itself, innately complete in all its potential,
Is conceived in uncontrived naturalness.
Yet you sophists, who take the two truths literally,
Distort being itself with your logic and analysis.
How long your journey, you followers of awakening-being philosophy!

While mind itself doesn't take up the good or give up the bad,
A meticulous practice of purity acts as an added pollutant.
With the forms of dualistic fixation you distort what is not two.
You seek a sublime state where there is nothing to be attained.
How elegant you are, you followers of ritual philosophy!

In experience itself, which doesn't become better or worse,
The conventions of outlook, practice and behavior fall away.
Yet, because of your investment in intelligent and skillful action,
The way you think leads you astray: you act when there is nothing to be done.
How tiring your chosen disciplines, you followers of behavioral tantra!

No outside, no inside and nothing in between — that quality of attention is
Mind itself, free from conceptual distortions.
Yet your thinking creates symbols for what is profound and clear.
How ineffective, you followers of union philosophy!

Effort and potential don't affect how mind is.
It is what it is: you ride the result.
While complex practices may restore vitality to mind, channels and energy,
How tiring they are, you followers of similar union!

Mind itself has no heads, hands or regalia.
Seeing what arises as a deity's form, or hearing sounds as a mantra —
Such fixed notions lead you astray.
You won't see mind itself through the path of great union!

ཀྱི་དོ༔
ང་ཡི་རང་བཞིན་རྟོགས་པ་ཆེན་པོ་ལ༔
འཁོར་འདས་ཆོས་རྣམས་སྣང་སྟེ་གྲོལ་བར་རྟོགས༔
མན་ངག་གནད་རྣམས་རང་གྲོལ་ཆེན་པོར་རྟོགས༔
ལྟ་བའི་གནད་རྣམས་དཀའ་ཚད་མེད་པར་རྟོགས༔
སྒོམ་པའི་ལམ་རྣམས་འབད་རྩོལ་མེད་པར་རྟོགས༔
སྤྱོད་པའི་ཆོས་རྣམས་གནད་བཀག་མེད་པར་རྟོགས༔
འབྲས་བུའི་དོ་པོ་ཡིད་སྨོན་བྲལ་བར་རྟོགས༔
རྟོགས་ཞེས་བུ་བཞད་བློས་བཏགས་ཚམ་དུ་ཟད༔
ཆོས་རྣམས་ཀུན་གྱི་དོ་པོ་བྱུང་ཆུབ་སེམས༔
སངས་རྒྱས་ཀུན་གྱི་ཐུགས་ཀྱང་བྱུང་ཆུབ་སེམས༔
སེམས་ཅན་ཡོངས་ཀྱི་སྒོག་ཀྱང་བྱུང་ཆུབ་སེམས༔
བྱུང་ཆུབ་སེམས་ལ་ཀུན་རྟོབ་དོན་དམ་མེད༔
མེད་ཅེས་སྨྲ་ནས་སྟོང་པར་རྒྱས་མི་གདབ༔
ཡོད་ཅེས་བཟུང་ནས་རྟག་པར་བློས་མི་འཆོས༔
མ་བཟུང་མ་བཏང་རང་གར་བློ་འདས་དབྱིངས༔
བསམ་ཡུལ་སློས་པ་ཀུན་དང་བྲལ་བའི་ཀློང་༔
ང་ལ་བཅོས་མའི་རྣམ་རྟོག་མེད་པའི་ཕྱིར༔
དགེ་སྡིག་ལས་དང་འབྲས་བུ་གདན་ནས་བྲད༔
ལྟ་སྒོམས་དེང་དེ་འཛིན་གྱིས་ཅི་ཞིག་བྱ༔
བསྐྱབས་པས་གྲུབ་པའི་སངས་རྒྱས་ང་མ་ཡིན༔
ང་ཡི་རང་བཞིན་ཀུན་ཁྱབ་ཆེན་པོ་ལ༔
ས་ལམ་བགྲོད་པས་མཐོང་བ་གལ་སྲིད༔
དེ་ཕྱིར་རེ་དོགས་འཕུར་བུར་མི་འཆིང་བར༔
ལྟ་བ་བཟང་པོའི་ངང་དང་ཕྱོལ་ལ་ཞོག༔
སྒོམ་པ་བཟབ་མོའི་ལུགས་ནས་ཕོན་ལ་ཞོག༔
སྤྱོད་པ་འཇུར་བུའི་རྒྱལ་འཆོས་ཤིག་ལ་ཞོག༔
འབྲས་བུ་ཆེན་པོའི་རེ་དོགས་བསྣུར་ལ་ཞོག༔

Timeless freedom in great completion

Wonder of wonders!

My nature is great completion.
Complete — in all experience, patterned or free, there is nothing to give up or attain.
Complete — all key instructions end up in utterly natural release.
Complete — all key outlooks end up in no conceptual position.
Complete — all paths of practice end up in making no effort.
Complete — all teachings on behavior end up in no do's or don't's.
Complete — the essence of result is to be free of hope.
And this term "complete" is just a concept, too.

Awakening mind is the essence of all experience.
Awakening mind is the heart of all awakened ones.
Awakening mind is the life force of all beings.
Apparent and ultimate are not found in awakening mind.

To say "it is not" does not make it empty.
To maintain "it is" does not make it solid.
It is a realm beyond thought — untroubled, nothing held, nothing dispelled —
A space free from the complications of thought and object.

Because I am free from the thinking that distorts experience,
The evolution of good and evil ends completely.
What are deities, mantras and absorptions meant to do?
I am not a wakefulness that comes from practice.
My nature is universal presence:
How can seeing come through paths and levels?

Therefore, having loosened the knots of expectations,
Let go of outlook's razor-edge and rest.
Step out of deep practice's cozy cocoon and rest.
Break out of behavior's constricting conventions and rest.
Throw away expectations for dramatic results and rest.

སྐྱེམས་དང་མི་སྐྱེམས་ལས་འདས་དུན་པའི་ངང་༔
བྱ་དང་མི་བྱའི་རྩིས་གདབ་དབྱིངས་སུ་ཡལ༔
སྤོང་དང་མི་སྤོང་ལས་འདས་བྱུང་རྒྱལ་སེམས༔
ཡོད་དང་མེད་པའི་ཕྱོགས་ཞིག་གཤུག་པའི་ཀློང་༔
སྐྱ་བསམ་བརྗོད་དུ་མེད་པའི་རིག་པ་ལ༔
དེར་འཛིན་གཉེན་པོ་མེད་པའི་སྤྱོད་ཡིང་ཅན༔
བཅེར་བུ་སྐྱིང་པ་རང་གྲོལ་སོ་མའི་གཤིས༔
འབད་རྩོལ་སྤོས་པ་ཀུན་དང་བྲལ་བའི་ཀློང་༔
དུས་གསུམ་འཕེལ་འགྲིབ་མེད་པའི་ངང་ལ་གནས༔
ཀུན་ཏུ་བཟང་པོའི་དགོངས་ཉམས་ལས༔
རྟོགས་པ་ཆེན་པོ་ཡེ་གྲོལ་སོར་གཞག་ཏུ་བསྟན་པའི་ལེའུ་སྟེ་གཉིས་པའོ༔

ཀྱེ་ཧོ༔
དེ་ལྟར་སྣང་སྲིད་ཐོབ་བྲལ་བའི་བྱུང་རྒྱལ་སེམས༔
བདེ་བར་གཤེགས་པ་རིག་པའི་སྟེང་པོ་ཅན༔
རྒྱུད་ལ་གནས་ཀྱང་བཙོས་མའི་ཞེན་གྱིས་བཅིངས༔
ཇི་ལྟར་སྐྱོམ་བཞིན་སྐྱིད་པོའི་དོན་ལ་སྒྲིབ༔
རྩ་བྲལ་དོ་པོ་མེད་པའི་ཚོས་ཉིད་ལ༔
ཤེས་བྱ་སྐྱེ་འགགས་མེད་པར་སྒྲོ་བཏགས་པས༔
གཟུགས་མེད་གཟུགས་སུ་བཙོས་པ་ཇི་བཞིན་དུ་
རྒྱལ་བའི་དོན་ལས་གཡོལ་བ་ཉིད་རེ་མོངས༔
འགའ་ཞིག་དུན་བསམ་འཕྲོ་འདུ་ཅད་པའི་རྗེས༔
ཆེད་འཛིན་གཉེན་པོས་བསྒྲུབ་པའི་སྟོང་སྐྱོམ་གཟུགས༔
འབད་པས་གཏུར་གྱིས་སྐྱོམ་པས་ལ་ཞང་ཅད༔
སྟོག་རྩར་ལས་རྒྱུད་འཇུག་པའི་གེགས་སུ་ཆེ༔

Practice or not practice — attention goes beyond.
Act or not act — decisions melt away.
Empty or not empty — awakening mind is beyond.
Be or not be — there is a vastness wherein
These differences fade away.

Awareness — not a word, not a thought, no description at all —
Has as its axis no corrective, no holding a position.
Its nature is bare, steady, fresh and unfolding,
A vastness free from all effort and complications.
Rest where there is no change or time.

The elimination of errors

Wonder of wonders!

Thus, awakening mind, in which there is nothing to give up or attain,
This buddha nature, which is awareness and peace,
Is present in you. Still, it is trapped in a cage of inventions.
Any notion of practice clouds the heart of the matter.

No origin, nothing there: that's just how it is.
Perception doesn't arise or vanish.
When you make it more than that,
It's like making form out of what is formless:
You lose touch with what is natural. How reactive you become!

Some people cut off the ebb and flow of thoughts and feelings
And construct an emptiness practice contaminated by goal-seeking.
Their forced and constricted practice wears them out.
Serious problems develop when reactive energy enters the life channel.

ལ་ལ་རྒྱལ་མའི་དོ་པོ་མ་མཐོང་བཞིན༔
རྒྱལ་མའི་ཚིག་གིས་བསླུས་པའི་ཡུང་མ་བསྟུན༔
དུན་བསམ་ཆོག་ཏུ་གྱུར་པའི་གདི་མུག་ལ༔
བློམ་གྱི་དོ་པོར་འཛིན་པ་ཞིག་ཏུ་འབྱུལ༔
ཁ་ཅིག་འགྱུ་དུན་སེམས་སུ་ཤེས་པའི་བློས༔
དུན་བསམ་འཕྲོ་འདུའི་ཕྱི་ལ་རྒྱམ་རྟོག་ཅིང་༔
སྐྱེ་འགག་གནས་སུ་འདེབས་པའི་བསམ་གཏན་དེས༔
ལོ་བརྒྱར་བསྒོམས་ཀྱང་འཁྲུལ་པའི་འཁོར་ལོར་འཁྱུན༔
ཕལ་ཆེར་ཚོལ་སྒྲུབ་གོ་ན་དགར་ལངས་ཏེ༔
བསྒོམ་ན་མི་བདེ་སྣ་ཚོགས་རྗུག་ཏུ་ཡུང་༔
མ་བསྒོམས་རང་དོ་མ་ཤེས་འཁྲུལ་པར་འབྱམས༔
དེས་ཀྱང་མ་བཙོས་རྒྱལ་མའི་དོན་ལ་གཡེལ༔

ཀྱེ་ཧོ༔
དེ་ཀུན་སོ་སོའི་རྣམས་ལས་མི་འདའ་བས༔
ད་ནི་བློམ་དང་མི་བློམ་གཉིས་ཀའི་བློ༔
བཙོས་མའི་རྒྱམ་རྟོག་ཡིན་པར་དེས་བྱས་ཏེ༔
ད་ལྟའི་སེམས་ལ་བསྒྱུར་བཀོད་མེད་པར་ཞོག༔
དེ་ཡང་འདུ་བྱེད་བློ་ཡིས་འཚོལ་འདྲོ་དང་༔
བདག་བཞག་ཆེད་འཛིན་མཐའ་དག་སྤངས་བྱས་ནས༔
ཐད་ཀའི་ཤེས་པ་རྗེས་མེད་རང་འན་འདི༔
བཅས་བཙོས་བྱི་བསྒྱུན་སྤངས་ལ་རང་སོར་ཞོག༔
དེ་ཚེ་མཚན་མའི་རྒྱམ་རྟོག་ཅི་ཤར་ཡང་༔
གང་འར་མི་ལྟར་མཁན་དོས་བཟུང་ལ༔
སྤང་ལ་བླི་ཕུར་བཏབ་པ་བཞིན་དུ༔
ཤེས་རིག་རང་ཚོ་བཟུང་བ་གནད་དུ་ཟབ༔

Some just do not see what is naturally present.
Misled by what is said about presence, their practice is ineffective.
They take as the essence of practice a dullness
That suppresses thoughts and feelings. They are very confused.

Some who know that movement and memory are mind
Mull over the traces as thoughts and feelings ebb and flow:
They track the arising and fading of thinking. With this meditation,
Even if they practice for a hundred years, they just spin in confusion.

In general, work and effort by themselves create opposition.
If you practice, you stir up all sorts of pains and discomforts.
If you don't practice, you don't see what you are and wander in confusion.
In either case, you lose touch with what is straightforward and natural.

Wonder of wonders!

Because these errors stop you from going beyond ordinary experience,
Be clear that the approach of practice versus not practice
Relies on an artificial distinction. Without trying to reshape it in any way,
Rest in what you experience right now.

When you give up your reactive checking,
Managing and goal-seeking — all of it —
There is a direct knowing, open and free.
Stop changing or altering it. Rest right there.

Then, when conceptual thinking arises,
Don't look at what arises: be what knows the arising.
Like an oak peg in hard ground,
Stand firm in awareness that knows,
And go deep into the mystery.

ཇི་ལྟར་གཞིས་ཀྱི་གནས་ཚུལ་རྟེན་པ་ལ༈
འགྲོ་འོང་འཕེལ་འགྲིབ་མེད་པར་གནས་ན་ཡང་༈
དེར་འཛིན་གཉེན་པོའི་གཟེབ་དང་མ་བྲལ་ན༈
ཡིད་དཔྱོད་ཐེག་པའི་གནས་ལུགས་དག་ཏུ་གོལ༈
དེ་ཕྱིར་ལྷ་སྐོམ་སྒྲུབ་པའི་ཐ་སྙད་ཀུན༈
རྣལ་མའི་དོན་ལ་བློ་ཡི་སྤྲུན་པ་སྟེ༈
དུན་འཛིན་ཚུལ་བའི་གཉེན་པོ་དབྱིངས་སུ་ཤུབ༈
ཡེངས་དང་མ་ཡེངས་མེད་པའི་བཅལ་ཞུགས་ཅན༈
སྒོ་བསྲུ་བསལ་བཞག་མེད་པའི་རང་ཨན་པ༈
འབད་རྩོལ་སློས་པ་ཀུན་ལས་འདས་པའི་དབྱིངས༈
བསམ་དང་བསམ་བྱེད་མེད་པའི་གདེར་ཆེན་པོ༈
གདོད་ནས་སངས་རྒྱས་མེད་པར་ཤེས་པ་དེ༈
འདོད་པ་ཡེ་ནས་ཟད་པའི་ཆོས་ཉིད་ཅན༈
འཁོར་བའི་རྩ་དྲུལ་བའི་བྱུད་ཆོས་ཀྱིས༈
མུ་ཨན་དབྱིངས་སུ་སངས་པའི་གུ་ཡངས་པ༈
བདེན་རྟེན་མཐའ་ལས་འདས་པའི་སྟོང་པ་ཉིད༈
ཕར་གོལ་རང་གོལ་ཆེར་གོལ་ཆེན་པོའི་དོན༈
རྟོགས་ན་སངས་རྒྱས་ཀུན་དང་གཉིས་སུ་མེད༈
ང་དང་ཁ་དད་མེད་པར་སངས་རྒྱའོ༈
རྟེན་དུས་གསང་བ་ཆེན་པོའི་མན་ངག་གནད༈
ཡིད་དཔྱོད་ཐེག་པའི་གཞུང་དང་འདྲེས་པའི་ཚོ༈
ང་དང་གཉིས་སུ་མེད་པའི་རིག་འཛིན་གྱིས༈
ང་ཡི་དགོངས་པ་གཏན་ལ་འབེབས་པར་བྱེད༈
རིགས་གསུམ་སེམས་དཔའི་རྣམ་སྤྲུལ་ཚོས་འདིའི་བདག༈
ལས་འཕྲོ་སྐལ་བ་ཅན་གྱིས་སྤྱོད་པར་ཤོག༈
ཀུན་ཏུ་བཟང་པོའི་དགོངས་ཉམས་ལས༈
གོལ་ས་བཅད་པའི་ལེའུ་སྟེ་གསུམ་པའི་བདག་ཉིད་ཅན་གྱིས་རྟོགས་སོ༈

Even in this experience of naked presence
In which there is no movement or change,
If you don't avoid the mire of position-based correctives,
You lose your way in analysis and speculation.

All the conventions of outlook, practice and behavior
Are, in terms of what is natural, just intellectual chaff.
Let correctives aimed at attention subside into space.
With the chosen discipline of not being concerned about wandering,
Just let things be — don't change anything at all.
In a space beyond all complications and effort
Lies a great treasure — no thought, no thinking.

To know that from the beginning there is no awakening
Is to be where wanting has never been.
With this special teaching that rots the roots of samsara,
Wake up from the realm of misery.

When you open and relax,
There is an emptiness that goes beyond true or false.
Here, if you know arising release, natural release and direct release,
You are no different from all the awakened ones.
You are awake and no different from me.

In this age of strife, these vital instructions for the great mysteries
Are mingled with the canonical writings of the analytic approach.
A knowledge-holder who is not different from me
Will make my revelations clear.

Embodiments of the awakening beings of the three families, masters of
    this teaching,
And those blessed with natural talent, enjoy and make use of it.

Commentary

Eight conceptual approaches

This first section is a bit like a song. In each verse, whether with irony or exaggeration, Jigmé Lingpa pokes fun at how beliefs and conceptual fixations lead us astray in our practice. All that is missing is a chorus for us to sing while we laugh at our foolish earnestness.

Buddhism has often been called a religion of lists, and this section is based on one such list—the nine paths of the Nyingma tradition. This sequence reveals an internal coherence and order to the bewildering variety of practices in Tibetan Buddhism. Taken literally, these verses seem to be critical of the first eight approaches to practice. Another way for us to read this section, however, is that Jigmé Lingpa is using the first eight approaches as a series of metaphors to point out how conceptual approaches lead us away from what we are seeking to know through direct experience. When I look at my own experience over the years, I can see how I fell into each of the traps that he describes here.

Numbers, numbers, numbers... While this section is based on the nine-path framework, it contains eleven verses and is entitled "Eight conceptual approaches." How does it all add up?

The first verse is an introduction to the whole poem. Jigmé Lingpa begins with *mind itself*, a synonym for the non-conceptual awareness that he describes in this poem. He also makes the disclaimer that even though metaphors and words are not adequate for the task at hand, these are the methods he is going to use.

The second verse describes the quandary of ordinary knowing, that is, what happens when we are not aware of our potential for non-conceptual knowing. The next verse describes our plight when we relate to life through lopsided belief systems.

Jigmé Lingpa then goes through the first eight of the nine approaches to practice. In each verse, he contrasts the simplicity and directness of great completion with the confusion and problems that arise when practice is based in conceptualization or abstraction.

The first of the eight conceptual approaches is the *listener* (Skt. *shravaka*). As listeners, we listen to teachings and from what we hear, we learn how to refine attention until it becomes stable and clear. Stable clear attention gradually evolves into insight into the nature of experience. The result of this path is that we become progressively less reactive and come to know directly that the sense of self as a fixed entity has no basis.

Next is the path of the *independent buddha* (Skt. *pratyekabuddha*). In this path we rely on our own abilities. Motivated by the inevitably of death, we come to appreciate the interdependence of everything we experience. Through this understanding, we see, like the listener, that the sense of self has no foundation, but we are not free of the conceptual mind because we continue to hold the idea that what we experience exists objectively.

The *awakening-being* (Skt. *bodhisattva*) path is characterized by compassion and emptiness: on the one hand, our intention is to release beings from the struggles they endure; on the other, we know the absolute groundlessness of experience. These two facets reflect the two truths that form the philosophical basis of this path — the truth of how experience arises (as a dream, as an illusion) and the truth of how experience is (groundless, empty).

The next six paths are different forms of tantric practice where *tantra* refers to a set of practices and associated texts that are based on the premise that our spiritual potential is an unbroken continuum. Tantric practice consists of uncovering possibilities for that potential to manifest and take expression in our lives.

In *ritual tantra* (Skt. *kriya tantra*), we use ritual to discover and give expression to this spiritual potential. We see the spiritual as something greater than us. It inspires awe and devotion. We make ourselves worthy and capable of communion with the spiritual through the creation of sacred space, self-purification and the precise observance and performance of offering and honoring rituals.

In *behavioral tantra* (Skt. *charya tantra*), we discover and connect with the spiritual through our daily activities. Here we see the spiritual as something that is present in our lives in everything we do, more as a friend or companion than as something inaccessibly superior to us. This path leads to a more intimate relationship with the spiritual as it takes expression through the skill and intelligence we bring to our lives.

These next four approaches describe a clear progression from an initial connection with the possibility of groundless experience to the full experience of groundlessness itself.

Union tantra (Skt. *yoga tantra*) marks the transition from an external form of practice (working through ritual and behavior) to an internal form of practice (working directly with what arises in experience). In order to facilitate this transition, the profound and clear openness or emptiness of mind is given symbolic expression as a deity. We see the deity as a symbol of how we aspire to experience life, and practice consists of engaging life that way.

In *great union tantra* (Skt. *mahayoga tantra*), we imagine that we are the deity and that we are experiencing life as the expression of appearance-emptiness, sound-emptiness and awareness-emptiness. This path is the first interior tantra, interior because we are looking inside for understanding.

In *similar union tantra* (Skt. *anuyoga tantra*), we use energy-transformation methods to generate experiences that are similar to awakening. As we become familiar with these experiences and as our mind and body become deeply at ease, there is a greater likelihood that conceptual knowing just drops away.

These are the eight approaches referred to in the title for this section. In this poem, Jigmé Lingpa reverses the usual order for *great union tantra* and *similar union tantra*, but I have not been able to discern why he does so.

The ninth approach is *supreme union tantra* (Skt. *atiyoga tantra*). In this approach, we let go of any idea of awakening as something to be achieved, whether through the intermediary of a deity or through the generation of special experiences. Instead, we start from the premise that we are awake already and that there is nothing to be done. Practice consists of letting mind (the way we experience life) untie itself until there is no separation between the experience of life and what we are. There is no verse in this section about *supreme union tantra* because it is the subject of the rest of the poem.

Verse 1.1

Once known, mind itself is like space.
The nature of space is that there is nothing that is space.
In the same way, examples cannot really point out awareness.
Yet I rely on such methods to shed light on key points.

One summer day, two boys were throwing a ball back and forth. One asked, "Here we are playing, and the earth holds us up. But what holds the earth up?"

"I asked my dad about that a few days ago," said the other, "and he said that the earth is held up by four elephants, one in each of the four directions." They returned to their play.

A few minutes later, the first boy asked, "What holds the elephants up?"

"I asked my dad that, too, and he said that they stand on the shell of a giant turtle."

They threw the ball back and forth again. Then the first boy asked, "What holds the turtle up?"

The second boy stopped playing. He thought for a while and finally said, "I think it's turtles all the way down."

When you experience mind itself, it is turtles all the way down—infinite space without center or periphery.

In both mahamudra and dzogchen instruction, two of the direct-awareness traditions in Tibetan Buddhism, a distinction is made between *mind* and *mind itself*. *Mind* refers to how we ordinarily experience life, filtered and distorted by reactive patterns. *Mind itself* refers to a knowing, an openness, present in every moment of experience—an open knowing free from distortions and projections. A similar distinction is made between *experience* and *experience itself*, where *experience* refers to the content of experience and *experience itself* refers to the experiencing of what arises.

Mind itself is not a thing. There is an experience of vast openness and transparent awareness, an experience so vivid and intense that practitioners are often moved to say, "There is nothing there." The sense of "nothing there" pervades everything we experience, even as we see and hear the world around us, even as thoughts and feelings arise. Jigmé Lingpa uses the simile of space. Space is just there, whether there are objects or not. In this way it is like silence or stillness. Silence is present whether there is sound or not. Stillness is present whether there is movement or not. The same holds for this awareness: it is there whether thoughts, feelings or sensations are there or not. Like space, silence or stillness, it is there — yet there is no thing there.

Space is a simile, an analogy. Jigmé Lingpa is not presenting a fact or even a theory about mind or reality. He is describing his experience, an experience so vivid and meaningful to him that it is the basis of his life. Because he cannot put the experience into words, he uses the simile of space.

Any comparison carries the danger of giving us an idea, a picture, something we can hold on to in our minds. We easily fall into the illusion that we understand mind itself or awareness when we understand the example, but understanding an example is not the same as experiencing awareness directly. As Jigmé Lingpa says, *examples cannot really point out awareness*. With these words he is also saying that he is not trying to communicate a conceptual understanding of awareness. An analogy with music is helpful. A composer does not try to communicate a conceptual understanding of her music. Her intention is that we experience something when we listen to her music. In the same way, Jigmé Lingpa wants us to experience something when we read this poem.

Pay attention to what happens in you when you read *The nature of space is that there is nothing that is space*. You may experience a shift, a letting go. If you do, rest right there. Do not try to explain it to yourself or describe it in words. Just rest right there. That is the way to read this poem.

As you read the following verses and their commentaries, pay attention to what you experience. When Jigmé Lingpa writes *Yet I rely on such methods to shed light on key points*, he is saying that he is going to use words, examples and analogies to point to something, something that can be experienced but cannot be described or explained in words. As has been said in Buddhist writings, we often mistake the finger (the conceptual meaning of the words) for the moon (the shift in experience) to which the finger points. This poem is about those shifts.

Verse 1.2

> What is it like when a poor man has
> A priceless treasure in his home
> But doesn't know it? Just as he remains poor,
> You remain entangled in a net of unaware thinking —
> How heartbreaking, you beings, benighted in samsara!

In this verse, Jigmé Lingpa refers to a traditional Indian story about a poor man who journeys the world over in search of a treasure he has heard about. He eventually meets a sage in a remote mountain wilderness who tells him to take care of a tree behind his house. He returns to his home and discovers that the tree is dying. When he digs at the roots to see what the problem is, he uncovers a chest full of gold.

In all the great contemplative traditions it is said that when we are able and willing to rest in exactly what we are experiencing, however difficult it may be, we discover possibilities we did not know were there.

Take a recent experience, any experience that is strong and vivid — one in which you were deeply troubled or upset or one in which you were wonderfully happy and joyful. Open to the memory of that experience, rest there and ask, "What is this?"

When we rest and look, we first become aware of a mass of unaware thinking. These movements in mind have many layers — bodily sensations that both trigger and are triggered by thinking; reactive emotions that spill into thinking and other bodily sensations; beliefs, prejudices and ideals; emotional projections, agendas and interpretations — stories upon stories upon stories. As we continue to rest, we may touch uncomfortable and difficult feelings. As we rest further, we often find uncomfortable and difficult bodily sensations connected with those feelings. We may also encounter feelings of extraordinary physical or emotional well-being and the impulse to hold on to them. We may experience clarity and dullness or peace and turmoil, coming and going without any rhyme or reason. All these experiences are piled on top of each other and interwoven in a chaotic, bewildering muddle. The truly surprising discovery is that when we stop trying to sort out the muddle, when we stop trying to change it, when we stop trying to make sense of it — when we stop struggling with what we are experiencing and just experience it — attraction, aversion and indifference to what we are experiencing drop away and a space opens up. In that space we discover a possibility that we did not know was there and could not have imagined. For some, the possibility is the possibility of a profound peace; for others, it is more a transparent clarity or an intimation of limitless freedom; for still others, it is a sense of oneness, of no separation. Whatever its tone or however it arises, this is the priceless treasure we did not know was ours.

In other words, it is in knowing our own experience through and through that we discover the possibility of freedom. This knowing is not a psychological understanding of why we do things, what motivates us or the structure of our reactions. That kind of understanding may arise in the process, but it is a side effect. Nor does this knowing necessarily make us a better person, whether in the eyes of the world or in our own eyes. Such changes may arise, but again, as a side effect of our efforts. What we do come to know is that suffering comes from our wanting things to be different from what they are and from our struggling to change them. That understanding naturally brings us to feel compassion for others. This compassion is not based in pity, mercy or charity. It comes because we know, through our own experience, that we are all doing the same thing — struggling with our experience of life because we want things to be different from what they are.

As we continue to rest in what arises in experience, we discover the extraordinary possibility of being completely at peace — with our minds and hearts clear and open — no matter what we are experiencing. We see that everyone has the potential to experience their lives this way. Our hearts break, then, because we see and know the pain of the world, and we know at the same time that it does not have to be this way. In the face of the tragedy of the human condition, it is as if we have no skin — no barrier between the world and us. Compassion now takes on a different quality. It is no longer a feeling. It is how awareness, which is simultaneously freedom, peace and clarity, takes expression in our lives.

Verse 1.3

What is it like when you turn your back on the natural path?
Because you are enthralled by mistaken beliefs,
Your puritanical practice is lopsided,
Based as it is on some flawed metaphysical theory —
How reactive you are, you irrational extremists!

From the dzogchen point of view, all we have to do is sit, rest and do nothing, and let our confusion sort itself out, until the way we experience life becomes clear, empty and free. This way of practice sounds simple, but it is not easy, if only because the conditioning that prevents us from knowing this clarity and freedom is so very powerful. To be able to rest in whatever arises in experience, we need three qualities: the willingness to do so, the skill or know-how to meet what arises and the capacity to be present in what we experience without becoming lost in it.

Ajahn Chah says, "If you want to practice meditation, put a chair in the center of a room. Sit in the chair and see who comes to visit." Most of us do not have sufficient willingness, skill or capacity to let the visitors come and go on their own, like thieves in an empty house. Instead, we hold dearly to our ideas about what should or should not be happening and how things should or should not be. We often reduce everything to a single principle, a single perspective, in order to have an anchor, a reference point around which to organize everything we encounter in life. Here are some examples: "There is in me an entity (a soul) that does not change throughout time." "I think, therefore I am." "I am one with the universe." "I exist independently of what I experience." "I am nothing more than the electrochemical processes in my brain and body." "I am an instrument of God's will." "I am an illusion." "I am what I experience." "I am the author of my life." "I can attract whatever I need by an act of will." None of these principles is ultimately true, of course, but all of them (and many others) have been the fundamental tenet of at least one system of thought or religion.

Each of these metaphysical views gives us something to believe in. The belief provides us with a way to define what we are and, just as importantly, what we are not. Anything that contradicts our belief or even calls it into question we regard as wrong or not true. Conversely, we regard as right or true anything that reinforces or corroborates what we believe. Over time we become increasingly rigid and reactive, often resorting to elaborate reasoning and irrational arguments to justify and defend our core belief. We do not notice that we have become more and more reactive and that everything we say and do is about defending our views or countering potential threats to them. Rarely are we aware of how irrational or extreme we have become.

In this section of this poem, Jigmé Lingpa does not give any instruction or guidance about how to remedy these problems. His approach is to rest in open awareness and let those beliefs, even the core beliefs, resolve themselves. For me, that approach was not possible, at least not right away.

First, I had to learn to recognize my lopsided, extreme or dead-end thinking. I noticed that when I used such words as *never, always, must* or *have to*, I could be pretty sure that a pattern had taken over the microphone. I have also learned that when I am being rigid and inflexible, I am usually in the grip of an emotional reaction. The rigidity is a compensatory reaction to an uncertainty I am not able or willing to experience.

As much as possible, whenever I hear myself use absolutes such as *never* or *always* or *must*, I now stop and open to what I am experiencing. Sometimes I start with the rigidity in my body and then include feelings and thoughts. Sometimes I start with the position I am holding, and then include the feelings and physical sensations associated with it. And sometimes I start with the emotional feelings, how justified I feel, and then include the thoughts and sensations. However I start, I keep resting and including until I am resting awake and aware in the whole mess. It does resolve itself — in its own way and on its own time — but that is not something I control or can make happen.

Verse 1.4

Mind itself, originally pure, is like space.
As long as you look for it with conceptual tools,
You are like a bug encasing itself in its own spit —
In your obsession, you turn your back on what is truly meaningful.
How worn out you must be, you listeners, from rejecting everything!

What does it mean to say mind itself is originally pure?

Recall what it is like to be stopped, completely stopped, by a painting, a piece of sculpture, a dance or a beautiful vista. For instance, in the Nelson-Atkins Museum of Art in Kansas City, Missouri, there is a life-size statue of Guanyin (Skt. *Avalokiteshvara*) carved from a single tree. The moment I walked into the gallery and saw it at the far end, everything in me stopped. The sense of *I* as a separate entity vanished and everything became vivid and clear. Thoughts, feelings and sensations arose, but they came and went on their own. It was as if there was no movement — nothing to reject or attach to. Many people have a similar experience when they see Michelangelo's *David*, when they fall in love or when they lose someone close to them.

While one could take the phrase *originally pure* as a philosophical statement (and many have done so and built whole systems on it), it is more a description of an experience. The phrase was probably first used as a way to elicit a similar experience in the person who heard it. The more it was used, however, the more it became an idea, and then a concept.

Space is space. There is nothing that is space. In the same way, the sky is the sky. No matter what arises in it — violent hurricanes or typhoons, fog, sun, mist, clouds, snow, rainbows or the aurora borealis — the sky is still the sky. While you look at the sky, clouds and rainbows may form and dissolve. They appear out of nothing and dissolve back into nothing. The sky remains what it is — open clear space. Nothing defiles it, nothing sullies it, nothing debases it because there is nothing to define, sully or debase.

In the same way, no matter what thoughts, feelings or sensations arise, mind is mind, experience is experience and awareness is awareness. Thoughts, feelings and sensations arise out of nothing and dissolve back into nothing. The difference between the sky and awareness is that awareness is not something that we watch: awareness is what we are.

I spent a lot of time and effort in coming to understand the relationships between mind and awareness and experience. I reached a point where I could explain emptiness, compassion, non-duality, and many other concepts clearly to others. However, the explanations did not lead me anywhere, and I am not sure that they led anyone else anywhere, either. Explanations may be interesting, intriguing, enthralling and seductive, but in the end they are just a bunch of words and ideas. Some traditions hold that a sound conceptual understanding of non-self or emptiness is desirable, if not necessary, for effective practice. That may be true for some people, but I found that a conceptual understanding led me to a misleading sense of resting. Like a bug that uses the spit it secretes to encase itself, I ended up encased in my own conceptual understanding. I was resting in an idea. I was not resting in my physical body.

The more we hold on to a conceptual understanding of non-self or emptiness, the more we reject the thoughts, feelings and sensations that arise in our experience. We reject them because they intrude on our idea of emptiness. Emptiness has become a thing to us. It is a bit like rejecting wind, fog, rain, rainbows or mist because they intrude on the sky. We are caught up in our idea of how emptiness or non-self or original purity should be and do not experience how it is.

The best possible outcome from all this effort is that we give up because our efforts have left us worn out, fed up and completely at a loss as to what to do. Not infrequently, there is a moment then when our thinking, along with our conceptual understanding, collapses. In that collapse, other possibilities open.

This path is not about preferring one experience to another, one feeling to another, but about being present in everything that arises. Nothing is rejected. Even in the most painful, most tragic or most repugnant experiences, the quality of awareness itself, the quality of being awake and aware, is still there, like the sky.

Verse 1.5

> Mind is the source of all experience, patterned or free.
> You wake up completely when you rest and do nothing at all.
> Instead, you are dogmatic and single-minded in your belief
> In the teachings of ignorance, interdependence and samsara.
> How pleased you must be, you self-reliant ones, with your artificial awakening!

Mind is the source of all experience. When we encounter an awe-inspiring vista or listen to beautiful music, it is mind. When we are upset and frustrated because we cannot find our car keys, it is mind. When we are angry, greedy, proud or envious, it is mind. When our hearts are filled with love and compassion, it is mind. When we see things clearly and know exactly what to do, it is mind. When we are lost in confusion, depression or grief, it is mind. When we feel clear, alive and awake, it is mind.

Mind is not a thing. When all the pieces are in place — a flower, light, our eyes open and directed at the flower — the experience of seeing a flower arises, seemingly out of nothing. When we look away, the experience of seeing the flower vanishes. The experience of seeing the flower does not go anywhere. It just disappears. Where is the experience of seeing then? We cannot say. It is not inside or outside or in between. Yet the experience of seeing is itself clear and vivid.

When we look at a flower, its color and shape are just there. We do not have to do anything to bring them into experience. When music strikes our ears, the melody and tones are just there. It is the same with the other senses — taste, touch and smell. Thoughts, emotions, feelings, ideas, judgments, prejudices, stories, and insights arise — unbidden, unpredictable, welcome, unwelcome, comforting, disturbing, familiar, strange — and it is all mind. Mind is the source of everything we experience.

To be awake and present we do not have to do anything. If we rest and do nothing at all and just experience whatever arises, the awake quality of mind is naturally present. Practice consists of recognizing that quality, keeping in touch with it and trusting it. This is the subtle, and subtly difficult, instruction that Jigmé Lingpa describes in the second section of this poem. The greatest challenge is to develop the willingness, skills and capacity to be able to rest and do nothing at all. A big part of that challenge is to learn and to trust that resting is all that is needed.

Most of us find the complete lack of ground difficult — difficult to see, difficult to take in, difficult to fathom and difficult to accept. Much has to change before we can experience life this way.

When we rely only on our own understanding and do not have the guidance, the encouragement, the inspiration or the experience of someone who has traveled these paths, we usually turn away. We turn away because we are unable to face that infinite depth in ourselves, the complete absence of any ground to experience. Instinctively we reach out for a structure, a framework, a way to understand what we are experiencing. For some people, that framework may be the ideal of union with a cosmic self. For others, it may be a nihilistic denial of the reality of everything that we experience.

Where better to turn than the teachings on ignorance, interdependence and *samsara,* the cycle of existence? These teachings are the core of all traditions of Buddhism — thoroughly tested and refined over centuries of philosophical reflection and contemplative practice. They appear to provide a reliable map of the human condition, complete with directions and a guidebook for the path to enlightenment or nirvana. We adopt this framework and use it as a base for our spiritual practice. It makes sense to us and we come to believe it, and that is where the problems start.

Faith, at least the way I use the word, is the willingness to open to experience, whatever it is, however pleasant or unpleasant, however difficult or challenging, and let it unfold and resolve itself. In the process, it extends, deepens or wakes us up to possibilities. Belief, on the other hand, is how we interpret what arises in experience to confirm and reinforce what is already inside us. The one opens, the other closes. Faith, whether in a teacher, a teaching, a text, a ritual or a practice, all too easily decays into a set of beliefs, and those beliefs then become the organizing principle of our lives.

When confronted with the openness and groundlessness of experience, of mind, of awareness, it is only human to reach for something solid. We take what brought us to that openness, what inspired us, and now use it to confirm our understanding, our sense of who we are and our place in the world. And that is what often happens with the teachings on ignorance, interdependence and samsara. The map gives us a way of understanding the world, life and ourselves. Bit by bit, it solidifies into a set of beliefs. We go about our lives, confident in our understanding of what it means to be awake. Unnoticed, ignored or forgotten, the groundlessness of experience slips away — out of sight, out of mind. Without noticing the change, we become rigid, brittle and defensive. We live in an idea of being awake, hold on to a feeling of being awake and increasingly avoid anything that threatens that idea.

It is difficult to let go of the idea of being awake because so much of our identity is wrapped up in it. What would we be if we did let it go? It is hard to let go of beliefs and harder still to let go of our ideas about who and what we are, particularly when we are pleased with our independence and self-reliance.

Verse 1.6

Mind itself, innately complete in all its potential,
Is conceived in uncontrived naturalness.
Yet you sophists who take the two truths literally
Distort being itself with your logic and analysis.
How long your journey, you followers of awakening-being philosophy!

The first two lines are more poetic than philosophical as the Tibetan text subtly alludes to one of the Twelve Deeds from the life of Buddha Shakyamuni — his entering the womb of his mother and being conceived. At the same time, the phrases *innately complete* and *uncontrived naturalness* are important terms, communicating qualities of the experience of mind itself. In that experience, all the possibilities and potentials of mind are seen to be already present and awareness is just there. It is not the outcome of any process — creative, developmental, constructed or generative.

Jigmé Lingpa is using high formal poetry to communicate his understanding and insights. In our own culture, we have largely lost touch with poetry that uses formal language and extended metaphors to express deep insights or experiences. We are not used to this form of expression. Perhaps the best place to start is a short exercise.

Sit for a few moments and open to everything you experience. Start with everything you see in the room in which you are sitting — the chairs, tables, desk, carpet, walls, paintings, lighting, ceiling and floor. Open to all the sounds you hear — the hum of appliances, the rumble of the furnace or air-conditioning, music if you have any playing, voices, and other sounds from neighbors or the street outside, the rustle of the wind, the patter of rain, the hush of snow. Open to all the physical sensations you experience, too — the feel of your clothes on your skin, the pressure of the chair against your body, any physical tensions or discomforts in your body. Include tastes and smells if there are any. Then include all the thoughts and feelings that are there as well.

Rest in the field of everything you experience, and then pose the question, "What experiences all this?" Do not try to answer the question. Just pose it and see what happens.

You may experience a shift. The knowing quality is heightened. It is sometimes reinforced by a sense of vastness or greater space. Rest right there. Granted, the shift may last only a moment or two before your awareness and attention collapse into thinking, but the shift gives you a taste of mind itself.

This knowing includes everything we experience — everything. Thus, the knowing is *innately complete in all its potential*. To say that it *is conceived* means that this knowing becomes evident in our experience when we rest in *uncontrived naturalness*, when we rest in exactly what arises in our experience — sensory sensations, emotions and thoughts — as well as the experience of being aware itself.

Experiences of this sort arise in different ways and to different degrees. Some people have to crawl through alligator-infested swamps or cross hot barren deserts to have even a glimpse of something like this. Others swim smoothly in this sea, riding the waves, and still others soar effortlessly in this sky. How such experience comes to us does not matter.

Once we have touched it, we are faced with an amazing paradox. On the one hand, we know that there is nothing there, not a thing. On the other, we experience a fullness of life we had not known was possible. The anonymous author of *F.O.A. — Full on Arrival* says it this way:

> Until we experience it,
> Emptiness sounds so
> Empty.
> Once experienced,
> All is empty by comparison.

This experience is so meaningful to us — it changes the way we experience life so profoundly — that we want others to know it. How do we communicate an experience that seems so paradoxical, so empty and groundless on the one hand, and so full and vivid and clear on the other? Our rational mind insists that we find a way to reconcile these two aspects.

We see that there have to be two truths. One says that there is nothing there, while the other says that things appear anyway. Now all we have to do is figure out the relationship between these two truths. Then we will have a solid philosophical explanation for what we experienced. Hundreds of years ago in India, Buddhist philosophers followed exactly this line of reasoning. They struggled with the same question and developed several sophisticated explanations of the two truths and how they are related. These explanations have come down to us today.

Alas, the explanations do not work. Despite the carefully constructed arguments and flawless logic, other people do not have the same experience or do not understand ours. Because we still want to help them wake up to what we know to be true, we find subtler ways to explain and justify our analysis. We debate our formulations with others, constantly refining them, but more and more we are caught up in logic, analysis, definitions and arguments. Our original experience now seems like a distant and vague memory. Was it a dream? We have our philosophy, but much as we value it, it has no power. We have lost our original path and now wander along the pathways of the intellect, adding argument to argument, constructing sophisticated lines of reasoning that go nowhere.

As with those who fall into belief, the road back is long and difficult for those who rely on their intellects. How did we end up like this?

Verse 1.7

> While mind itself doesn't take up the good or give up the bad,
> A meticulous practice of purity acts as an added pollutant.
> With the forms of dualistic fixation you distort what is not two.
> You seek a sublime state where there is nothing to be attained.
> How elegant you are, you followers of ritual philosophy!

Time and again, when my teacher was teaching about mind itself, he would borrow someone's glasses. He would place one of the lenses on a piece of white cloth, then on a piece of black cloth and then on a piece of cloth with a pattern. He was pointing out that mind itself, this transparent open knowing, is not affected by what arises in experience—pain or pleasure, good or bad, pure or impure, one or many.

In order to experience that knowing, we need a level of attention that has two qualities. First, we are not caught up in the coming and going of thoughts and emotions. Second, we can experience thoughts and emotions as clouds forming and dissolving in the space of mind. This level of attention is not the same as the experience of being the watcher in which we observe the coming and going of thoughts. In the experience to which the phrase *mind itself* refers, we are the space and we are the thoughts at the same time.

Some people are able to generate that level of attention naturally. Others have to work long and hard before they can rest and experience mind this way. Practice does not change mind itself but it can and does interrupt, disrupt, wear away or break down the operation of reactive patterns and open the possibility of recognizing mind itself. Practice also builds the capacity in the clear, stable attention needed to stay in touch with mind itself once it has been recognized.

Ritual is one such method of practice. When we perform a ritual with attention, the imagery and symbolism in the ritual disrupt pattern-based projections. The steps of the ritual interrupt the formation of the world that patterns project. They break down how those projections manifest in our actions. Over time, patterns lose their momentum because the ritual prevents pattern-based reactions from building momentum. As the ritual repeatedly disrupts pattern-based experience, it opens up the possibility of clear non-conceptual knowing.

However, sometimes we take the purity associated with ritual as an end in itself. We strive to do the ritual perfectly, making sure that we achieve purity in every respect: we cleanse ourselves in the prescribed way; we wear the appropriate clothes cleaned in the appropriate way for the occasion; we dust, sweep, wash and decorate the ritual space exactly as prescribed; we unwrap and arrange the ritual utensils and whatever else the ritual calls for; we perform each step of the ritual precisely, perfectly, in a seamless flow; and so on, right up to the end when we again clean the ritual space and return the implements to their place of keeping. Because our aim is purity, we never let go of the conceptual mind. Instead, we are constantly observing, judging and criticizing our own performance and the performances of others. Once in the three-year retreat, my insistence on proper procedure during a complex and difficult ritual inspired one of the other retreatants to throw a heavy glass bowl at me. Fortunately it missed, but it put a good dent in the wall behind me. My focus on purity brought out a rigidity in me that I was not aware of until the glass bowl hit the wall.

While ritual is an important element in the practice of Tibetan Buddhism, Jigmé Lingpa is hardly advocating it here. With deliberate irony, he uses ritual tantra as a metaphor for the tendency to focus on elegance, correctness or purity and to overlook the natural transparency of mind itself.

Verse 1.8

In experience itself, which doesn't become better or worse,
The conventions of outlook, practice and behavior fall away.
Yet, because of your investment in intelligent and skillful action,
The way you think leads you astray: you act when there is nothing to be done.
How tiring your chosen disciplines, you followers of behavioral tantra!

In direct-awareness practice, mind is often likened to space. Space is space. It is not something that becomes better or worse. To return to the example of the sky, weather does not make the sky better or worse. Winds come and go. Clouds form and disappear. Sometimes they grow into thunderstorms or hurricanes. Lightning flashes, thunder crashes and rain pours down. Later the sun shines, bathing the world in its warmth and light. Through it all, the sky does not become a better sky or a worse sky. It continues to be the sky. In the same way, life stirs up storms within us, brings us great joy and great sadness, pleasure undreamt of and heartache beyond bearing. These ups and downs do not affect experience itself. Can we be in what is arising, experiencing it in all its intensity, and be like the sky at the same time?

When we can, we experience such a profound freedom that the conventions of outlook, practice and behavior drop away. Present in the fullness of life, we no longer approach practice in terms of "This is the outlook that I hold, this is the practice that I do, this is the kind of behavior that supports and gives expression to this practice." That way of practicing is analogous to sounding out words when we are learning to read. We sound out the words as a way of learning the words and how to say them. We pay attention to outlook, practice and behavior in order to learn these different aspects of practice. When we know how to read, we stop sounding out words. We just read and take in the meaning. In the same way, when we are awake and present in the ups and downs of life, we do not think in terms of outlook, practice and behavior. We just live our lives.

A friend of mine, a Zen teacher with many years of experience, told me that she felt her practice was incomplete because she was feeling more than a little anxious at the prospect of her husband's coming brain surgery. She felt that she should be able to accept whatever happened with equanimity. Another colleague, again with many years of experience in practice and teaching, has a delightfully wicked sense of humor. At one point she insisted that she had to give up her sense of humor for the sake of practice. In both cases, I felt they were striving for an ideal behavior, an ideal that had little to do with being awake and present.

We are humans and we love those close to us, we care about them deeply and we experience pain and grief when we are separated from them. We feel anger toward those who hurt us or who hurt those close to us. The teachings of mind training and other practices show us how to use those feelings and how to use adversity (as well as good fortune) to deepen our relationship with life itself. For instance, in *The Thirty-Seven Practices of a Bodhisattva*, Tokmé Zongpo writes:

> When you are down and out, held in contempt,
> Desperately ill and emotionally crazed,
> Don't lose heart. Take into you
> The suffering and negativity of all beings — this is the practice of
>   a bodhisattva.
>
> Even when you are famous, honored by all
> And as rich as the god of wealth himself,
> Know that success in the world is ephemeral
> And don't let it go to your head — this is the practice of a bodhisattva.

These teachings do not tell us not to have feelings. They do not tell us not to cry. They certainly do not tell us not to laugh. These teachings tell us how to have feelings without being taken over by them. It is possible to come to a place where we genuinely feel love and caring for those who hurt or harm us. It is even possible to feel love and compassion for those who cause great suffering for others. Yet that love and caring, while they open up extraordinary possibilities, do not blind us to what needs to be done when problems arise.

Whether what we experience is wonderful beyond imagination or painful beyond belief, we are, at the same time, the sky. There is an openness and clarity in our experience that the conceptual mind cannot touch.

This way of being in the world, a way in which we experience but are not caught by happiness or unhappiness, gain or loss, respect or disdain, fame or obscurity, is not sought by everyone. When faced with the vast openness and utter groundlessness of such a life, of living moment to moment guided only by an open clarity, many people turn away.

Most of us rely on disciplines to guide us in how we live. Often, however, we become emotionally invested in those disciplines. They define who we are, particularly as to what we view as right and wrong and how we relate to the world. We may live a good and productive life because of the intelligence and skill we employ in practicing those chosen disciplines, but we are not free. Our emotional investment makes it difficult for us to let life unfold in its own way. Instead, we try to make life conform to our notions of right and wrong and we wear ourselves out from trying to control what we experience instead of just being in it.

Verse 1.9

No outside, no inside and nothing in between — that quality of attention is Mind itself, free from conceptual distortions.
Yet your thinking creates symbols for what is profound and clear.
How ineffective, you followers of union philosophy!

Over and over again we are told that all experience is mind, but many people have difficulty understanding what this means.

Take the experience of sight, for instance. We see a flower. Ordinarily we regard the flower as being outside us. It is "out there." Then we study Buddhism and run into lines such as "When you look at an object, there is no object: you see mind." Such instructions have generated a lot of confusion over the centuries as practitioners frequently have difficulty in understanding how what they see is mind. Their efforts usually leave them with only a conceptual understanding, as illustrated by the following story:

A monk had studied for many years and felt that he had come to a good understanding. He went to his teacher and said, "I'm ready to leave — to visit other monasteries and to test my understanding with other teachers."

The teacher nodded and said, "Very well. I'm not so sure, but I'll see you on your way."

At the main gate of the monastery, they said their farewells. Then, as the student was about to set off, his teacher called to him, asking, "Do you see that big boulder over there? Is it in your mind or outside your mind?"

Confident in his understanding, the monk replied, "It is in my mind."

"Ah," sighed his teacher, "you are going to have a difficult journey if you have to take that boulder with you. Perhaps you should stay and practice a bit more."

The confusion here is about perception. Do such instructions as "See objects as mind" mean that, in some way, those objects are in the mind? One way to clear up this confusion is to turn attention from what is seen to the seeing itself. When we look at a flower, we see the flower. When we look at a boulder, we see the boulder. In either case, where is the seeing?

When we look at the seeing itself, it is very difficult to say where it is. It does not seem to be outside, and it does not seem to be inside, either. It is definitely not between the two because it is not clear where "between" would be. Outside, inside or in between — these categories just do not seem to apply to the seeing itself. It is very curious. We have the experience of seeing, but we cannot say where that experience takes place. One might argue that the seeing takes place in the brain. That line of reasoning misses the point, however, because we do not experience seeing taking place in the brain.

When we look at the seeing itself, there is a shift, a heightened quality of just knowing. If we have sufficient stability in attention, we can rest in that shift. This knowing is not dependent on thinking or understanding. It is just knowing, and it is in the direction of mind itself — a groundless knowing free from the conceptual distortions of thinking.

In union tantra (Skt. *yoga tantra*), we form a connection with this groundless knowing through practices that involve imagining a deity. The deity is simultaneously seen as a symbol and an expression of open groundless clarity, as well as the embodiment of particular qualities. For example, Green Tara embodies compassion, power and protection. These qualities are expressed through the green color of her body (a combination of white, yellow and blue — the colors associated with peace, enrichment and power); through the gesture of generosity with which she holds her right hand; the blue lotus (a symbol of compassion) and the protection gesture of her left hand; and so forth. The groundless clarity is expressed through her appearing vividly and clearly out of absolutely nothing and dissolving back into nothing, like a cloud in the sky. The connection we make with her is experiential and emotional. It is not simply an academic or conceptual understanding.

Jigmé Lingpa points to a problem that often arises in this approach. Explicitly or implicitly, we come to believe in the magic of the deity and forget that it is both a symbol and an expression of mind itself. Our attachment to the sense of the deity as *other* keeps us in the conceptual realm and renders our efforts in practice ineffective.

The way out of the conceptual mind in deity practice is exactly the same as the way out with the flower or the boulder. Periodically, we shift attention from the form of the deity to ask, "Where is this experience? Where is the deity?" Thinking, even subtle thinking, stops for a moment, and we are back with mind itself.

Verse 1.10

> Effort and potential don't affect how mind is.
> It is what it is: you ride the result.
> While complex practices may restore vitality to mind, channels and energy,
> How tiring they are, you followers of similar union!

We talk again and again about how to let the mind rest; about how pain, discomfort, grief or anger disturbs the mind; or about what makes the mind dull or clear. However, this way of talking is misleading. Nothing actually affects the knowing that is the essence of mind. We cannot make it bigger or smaller, better or worse, clearer, duller, or more or less active. It is just what it is, a knowing that is empty, clear and transparent. Again, the analogy with space is helpful. Consider the space in the bowl of a wine glass, for example. We can fill the glass with water, wine or sand, but nothing we do actually alters the space in the bowl. Whether the glass is empty or full, the space formed by the bowl is just there.

The sutras of the Theravada and Mahayana traditions lay out various paths in which we develop certain specific qualities: faith, devotion, loving kindness, compassion, equanimity, patience and disillusionment with conventional life, to name a few. These qualities may interrupt and even break down the power and momentum of conditioning, but they do not change mind itself, this clear open knowing. While the potential for each of those qualities is present in us and, with a bit of effort, we can realize those potentials through practice, nothing we do changes the essential knowing of mind itself. In fact, when talking about mind itself, the word *potential* is itself misleading. It is like talking about the potential for space. What would that mean?

What happens when we stop trying to cultivate any potential? What happens when we stop trying to develop qualities that we think might be helpful? When I sit and let go of those efforts, there is a moment of sheer panic.

Because I am not doing anything, I do not know who I am and I do not know what to do. The panic is just the conceptual mind going into overdrive, of course, as it scrambles to hold on to something.

However, if I do not react to the panic, then I am left with just what I am experiencing. Whether I am distracted and confused or clear and present, what I experience is what I experience. As I sit this way again and again, the transparent knowing of mind itself becomes more evident. I have to be able to recognize it, of course, but it is there, whether I recognize it or not. When I recognize it, sitting has a different quality — an openness to what I am experiencing, a peace from knowing that I do not have to do anything with what I am experiencing, and a trust and freedom to be in what I am experiencing. In this way I ride the result, the transparent knowing of mind itself.

The tantras are based on the premise that this transparent knowing is just there, in every moment of experience. In similar union tantra, there are a number of meditation techniques whose aim is to heighten the clarity quality of attention to make it more likely that we will recognize mind itself. These techniques use visualizations, energy practices and physical exercises to generate similitudes of the transparent knowing of mind itself. The attention generated by these methods penetrates the projections of thought and emotion and opens the possibility that we just fall into the experience of mind itself.

One example is vajra recitation, in which the movement of the breath in the body is synchronized with the sounds of the syllables *om*, *ah* and *hung* to elicit deep states of relaxation and clarity. The practices of similar union tantra use meditations and physical exercises based on energy channels and vital essences in the body. Comparable methods are found in numerous disciplines, including yoga, martial arts and medicine. When practiced properly, they open up possibilities that are not ordinarily available to us. Energy transformation practices are, however, inherently dangerous because they work with the basic energies that sustain our lives and well-being.

Helpful and useful as these practices are, people can and do get caught up in the generation of higher and higher levels of energy and the associated experiences of bliss, clarity and emptiness. What was intended to help becomes, instead, a form of addiction. Other problems can develop. Because I did not know how to work with these higher levels of energy when I was in the three-year retreat, I developed debilitating physical problems and a quite serious depression. After the retreat, it took a good two decades of slow and patient work to recover from those mistakes.

To know the knowing of mind itself is no small matter. Some people are able to recognize and work with it easily. Others need years of effort to build up the necessary levels of attention to recognize this transparent knowing. It can take still more years to let patterns play themselves out to the point that we can recognize this knowing in everything we experience. In today's world, many people think that they can just let everything unfold on its own. Unfortunately, they often practice fruitlessly for years because they never develop sufficient stability and clarity in attention. They are constantly being swallowed by their own thinking, emotional reactions or confusion. Other people wear themselves out building skills, abilities and energy, but they never learn how to let go of the impulse to control what they are experiencing. They are not able to let experience unfold on its own. All of us have to face the questions of how much to work at building up abilities and how much to let go and be in what we experience. To what extent do we practice the path of potential? To what extent do we practice the path of result?

Verse 1.11

> Mind itself has no heads, hands or regalia.
> Seeing what arises as a deity's form, or hearing sounds as a mantra —
> Such fixed notions lead you astray.
> You won't see mind itself through the path of great union!

Probably no practice in Tibetan Buddhism creates as much confusion and frustration as deity practice. The frustration is not limited to Westerners. On one occasion, a group of us asked Dezhung Rinpoche about deity practice. He leaned forward, hunched his shoulders and scrunched up his eyes — mimicking intense concentration — while he gave a running commentary: "Deity practice is so difficult! You imagine the faces, the arms, the legs and all the regalia, one by one. When you have one clear, the others fall out of focus. You pull them back in. You keep trying, harder and harder. Bit by bit, the form becomes clearer. You have the whole deity, except for one toe. When you bring that toe in, the whole image collapses. Then you have a headache!" he said, leaning back in his chair and laughing.

A deity is an expression of mind itself, or to word it more loosely, the spiritual in us and in the world. By the spiritual, I mean a way of experiencing life that is beyond the ordinary; that is free of thinking and emotional reaction; that is clear and vivid, alive, awake and present; a way in which "I" and "other" are not separate. In the practice of *great union tantra*, the spiritual is given form as a deity. We use this representation to connect with the spiritual by suspending our habituated patterns and filling our minds with the symbols and magic of the deity.

Deity practice is a complex practice. In fact, it layers several complex tasks on top of each other. One task is to develop the ability to generate a clear image of the deity's form. In doing so, we develop clear, stable attention. The stability comes from generating a vivid, steady image — complete with all the faces, hands and regalia of the deity—in our imagination. The clarity comes from knowing that the deity's form appears like a rainbow—form without substance.

A second task is to connect with the symbolic quality of each aspect of the deity's form. A lotus flower, for instance, may symbolize compassion or the presence of the purity of mind itself in the swamp of samsara. A noose may represent the restraining of emotional reactions, and a dagger how attention can penetrate even the most unyielding conditioning. At a certain point, the symbolism becomes alive and we connect directly with the qualities represented.

A third task is to feel that you are the deity, to know in your own experience what it feels like to embody the expression of awakening that the deity represents. Avalokiteshvara, for instance, is the embodiment of awakened compassion. When I do this practice, I ask, "What is it like to be the embodiment of awakened compassion?" When I pose this question, everything changes — my relationship with my body, senses, feelings and the ordinary stream of thoughts that make up everyday experience. They do not go away, necessarily, but their importance and influence fade and something else comes into the picture, perhaps only for a few moments. In those moments, I sense another possibility—a way of knowing and being that is not limited to blind reaction and conceptual thinking, a way imbued with the qualities represented in the iconography of Avalokiteshvara, a way that presents me with tremendous challenges, yet a way in which I could be present and free.

Through these efforts, we are increasingly able to rest in stable, precise and clear attention. At the same time, we create a whole life in our imagination—a life in which we are born as the deity, welcomed and empowered by buddhas and bodhisattvas, and praised and honored by beings. As the embodiment of awakening mind we send light and offerings to all the buddhas and draw in all their power and energy and then send millions of emanations of our own form into every realm of existence to free all beings from their struggles and sorrows. We know that this whole life arises like a dream, arising out of nothing and dissolving back into nothing. This experiential understanding gives rise to insight, knowing directly the nature of experience. In other words, stability and insight, qualities that are seen as methods of practice in the Sutra traditions, are seen as results in the Vajrayana traditions.

The same holds for mantra. We repeat a mantra such as *om mani padme hung* over and over again, until it becomes so much a part of us that it replaces the stream of subtle thinking in our minds. When it does, we have a quiet mind, for that stream of thinking has gone, and with it, the susceptibility to being taken over by reactive emotions. The voices and sounds we hear do not elicit the same reactions as before. We hear the sounds—a bit like pebbles dropping into a still pond—but there is little or no reaction to them. Mantra recitation also generates energy that powers attention. As the mantra becomes part of us, all we have to do to cut through distraction and disturbance is recall it.

People often go astray in deity practice, thinking that the point of this practice is to experience themselves and the world as the deity and to use those abilities to control what happens in their lives. In doing so, they are, perhaps unwittingly, using deity practice to build and reinforce a subtler sense of self. Jigmé Lingpa points out that deity practice does not bring us into the direct experience, the "it's turtles all the way down" quality, of open and groundless knowing. Deity practice may help to build abilities and open new possibilities, but it is not an end in itself.

This verse concludes the first section of this poem. In these ten verses, Jigmé Lingpa has pointed out a series of problems encountered in spiritual practice. To do so, he used the metaphors of ten different approaches to practice, beginning with ordinary life and lopsided belief and continuing through the first eight spiritual paths according to the Nyingma tradition. We may feel that only a few of the problems he has pointed out here are relevant to us. In my experience, we are only fooling ourselves if we think so.

Many years ago, one of my students started practice on the six realms of samsara—god, titan, human, animal, hungry ghost and hell being. An aggressive businessman, he quickly saw his connection with the anger of the hell beings and the jealousy and competitive mentality of the titans. He just as quickly dismissed my suggestion that all six realms were present in him. Six months and many hours of meditation later, he ruefully acknowledged that, yes, all six were alive and well in him. He could see his pride, his need for security, his greed and desire, and how they all caused him no end of problems in his life.

In the same way, the tendencies Jigmé Lingpa describes here are in all of us, even though we may not see them right away. At any stage of practice reactive patterns may rear up and lead us to ignore the spiritual. We find ourselves inexplicably reverting to reactive ways of relating to life. We think about things too much and are trapped by our conceptual thinking, beliefs or identity. We are too self-reliant, or obsessively concerned with truth or purity or symbols. These tendencies are persistent: they do not go away by themselves.

We become free of these tendencies only when we are aware of them and are able to experience them as clouds forming and dissolving in the sky. When we can do that, we are in good shape to practice the no practice of great completion, and that is what Jigmé Lingpa turns to next.

Timeless freedom in great completion

In this section Jigmé Lingpa presents the possibility of a freedom that stands outside of time. The structure of this section is a bit like a concerto. The first verse states a theme boldly, in pounding great chords — complete, complete, complete.... These chords, however, have a structure of their own, weaving together two frameworks widely used in Tibetan Buddhism to summarize the essential points of a path of practice.

The second verse is a lyrical praise of the centerpiece of all mahayana practice — awakening mind, or *bodhicitta* — though here, awakening mind takes on tones and meanings quite different from those of its inception in Indian Buddhism.

The following verse focuses on the groundless ground of great completion and introduces a second theme: no conceptualization. The next three couplets elaborate this theme. Jigmé Lingpa makes it clear that the timeless freedom he is describing is not a result of evolution (karma), transformation (deity practice) or development (a progression of stages).

Jigmé Lingpa then turns to practice, or the practice of no practice. Again, he invokes the initial theme, the great chords of the two frameworks, urging us to wake up from the particular form of sleep that adherence to these frameworks could induce. In the last two verses, the concerto reaches a climax of utter simplicity and ends on a note of extraordinary promise.

Verse 2.1

Wonder of wonders!

My nature is great completion.
Complete — in all experience, patterned or free, there is nothing to give up or attain.
Complete — all key instructions end up in utterly natural release.
Complete — all key outlooks end up in no conceptual position.
Complete — all paths of practice end up in making no effort.
Complete — all teachings on behavior end up in no do's or don'ts.
Complete — the essence of result is to be free of hope.
And this term "complete" is just a concept, too.

Having pointed out how we can fall into conceptual confusion, no matter how sophisticated, subtle or potent a practice we pursue, Jigmé Lingpa turns to the no-practice practice of dzogchen or great completion. From the perspective of dzogchen, there is nothing to do, and in this first verse, he shows how doing nothing is the completion of every aspect of practice. For instance, instruction finds its completion in letting each and every experience release itself, that is, in doing nothing with what arises. Outlook finds its completion in letting go of any conceptual position, that is, in doing nothing with respect to outlook.

The structure of this verse is quite remarkable. What appears to be a straightforward set of reductions leads the reader through two carefully interwoven frameworks. The first framework is ground, path and result — what is going on, what do we do, where are we going — and applies to lines 2, 3 and 7. The second framework is outlook, practice and behavior — how do we view things, what do we work at, how do we live that — and applies to lines 4, 5 and 6. The two converge in line 7, and in line 8 — with a gesture reminiscent of Zen — he throws away the whole notion of completion.

My nature is great completion.

As in the first section, the voice is the voice of Ever-present Good (Samantabhadra). He is speaking in the first person and is describing how he sees and experiences practice and awakening.

Complete — in all experience, patterned or free, there is nothing to give up or attain.

Patterned experience is a free translation of *samsara* — how we experience the world when we are in the grip of emotional reactions. For instance, when we are angry, we see the world in terms of opposition. When we are greedy, we see the world as withholding what we need. *Free experience* is a similarly loose rendering of *nirvana*, those moments when we are not only free from the grip of emotional reaction, but our experience of life is so vivid and awake that the fullness of experience eliminates any sense of self or individuality. Ordinarily, we push away emotional reactions and hang on to those special moments, but the radical perspective of great completion is that each moment of experience, whether reactive or not, is complete in and of itself. In other words, everything we experience is just an experience. This is the ground of no ground in great completion, and it is the basis for the no-practice practice of doing nothing. Because all experience, patterned or free, is just experience, there is nothing to do to it — nothing to add, nothing to remove, nothing to increase, nothing to decrease, nothing to give up, nothing to attain.

Complete — all key instructions end up in utterly natural release.

As for path, it follows from the previous line about ground that the path of practice consists in not doing anything. If we do not do anything with or to thoughts when they arise — we do not follow them, we do not cut them off, we do not suppress them — they come and go on their own. For practice, then, we just allow experience to unfold on its own. Here is one way:

Put a cushion or a chair in the middle of a room or in a quiet place outdoors. Sit down and let your body settle comfortably. Then let your breath settle. If it helps, follow it carefully for a few breaths, but then just let it come and go on its own. Let your mind settle, too. One traditional instruction sums all this up as, "Body on the cushion, mind in the body, relaxation in the mind."

Now just sit there and do nothing.

Thoughts arise, of course, and some of them will catch you. I use the word *catch* because, when thoughts arise, I do not decide which ones I will follow and which ones I will just experience coming and going. Some thoughts, feelings and sensations simply come and go on their own and cause no disturbance. Others catch me and I fall into distraction. Which does which is not something I control. As soon as I recognize that I have been distracted, I am already back. There is nothing more to do but start again. A puff of wind, the sound of a siren, the pattern of light and shadow in front of me — they catch me. When I recognize that I have been caught, I am back and start again. Last night's dinner with friends, a harsh word to or from my partner, a mistake at work, a pat on the back — these also catch me. I come back and start again. I feel inadequate, that I should be doing more — I come back and start again. I am enjoying the feeling of peace — I come back and start again. Clarity or dullness, bliss or pain, no thoughts or madhouse, duality or non-duality, emptiness or fullness, whatever experience catches me, I come back and start again. Any feeling that I am finally getting somewhere, any feelings of pride, achievement, relief, joy, awe, or devotion — I come back and start again.

As my mind settles, something else begins to happen. I experience the play of emotional reactions — thoughts, feelings and associations — just coming and going. Specific thoughts, feelings and sensations catch me less frequently, even when they are powerful or intense. It is a bit strange to sit utterly at peace while my whole being seethes with anger, or to be completely at peace while I am feeling cut to the core by how someone has treated me. The intensity of the feeling suggests that there should be more disturbance, but the wonder is that it is possible to be completely at peace in powerful feelings and experiences, positive or negative, without being disturbed or distracted and without suppressing or controlling them. Bit by bit, I can let experiences of emptiness, transcendence or immanence come and go, too. They tend to catch me in a different way because, as Alexander Pope says, "Hope springs eternal in the human breast…"

Every experience lets itself go, whether it is pain in my leg, anger at an insult or slight, warmth for my family, rage at injustice, love for all who walk on this planet or the groundlessness of experience itself. Like the morning mist or a rainbow in the sky, every experience comes out of nothing and dissolves back into nothing.

Complete — all key outlooks end up in no conceptual position.

As soon as I take a position, I end up in a contradiction. I may say things exist, but they change and disappear before my eyes. It is very hard to pin down what actually exists. If I say things do not exist, I am confronted with a world of experience. If I claim that I hold no position, that statement itself is a position — an example of both an ancient and a postmodern dilemma. In other words, I am in a box.

If I take the box apart, it reforms while I am taking it apart. If I try to step out of it, I end up back in it, too, like Alice in *Through the Looking Glass*. If I try to understand it, I have accepted the world it defines and I am still in it. If I try to ignore it, I continue to live in the world it defines and I never leave it. If I try to change it, it is like drawing on water: what I do has no effect. If I try to rise above it, I find that I am tied to it and it pulls me back down. If I push against it, it simply pushes back. If I analyze it, the analysis, no matter how subtle or intricate, leads me back to where I started — the box.

It is as if the whole universe is wonderfully skilled in *reductio ad absurdum*. No matter what I do, my every effort is rendered meaningless, a situation that easily leads to a philosophy of despair.

How do I take no position, then? The only way I know to move in the direction of no position is to experience as completely as possible what is happening in me when I take or hold a position. Holding a position, any position, is a movement in mind and body, just like thinking, feeling and sensing. When I hold a position, there are subtle physical, emotional and cognitive tensions and contractions that I am often not aware of. If, when I become aware of holding a position, I move attention to the body, I can become aware of the physical tensions and contractions. Sometimes it works the other way round — I first become aware of tensions and contractions and then become aware that I am holding a position.

It is possible to rest there, just experiencing both the tensions and the holding of the position. Sooner or later, and the *when* is not up to me, something lets go. Often I am unable to say exactly what lets go. For a moment, I just experience what is there. The letting go, the release, is itself a movement in mind, and there are corresponding shifts and changes in the body. All I can do is experience what happens. The rest, as T. S. Eliot says in *Four Quartets*, is not my business.

Of course, if I sit down with the intention of letting something go, of getting out of the box, then I am back in the box. I can only be right there, in the experience of the box — open, clear and aware, to the best of my ability. I do not control what happens then, just as I do not control what happens in my life. To practice this way is not easy, and it can be more than a little frustrating. I hesitate to say that it works, whatever that might mean, but anything else puts me straight back in the box.

Complete — all paths of practice end up in making no effort.

The phrase *no effort* is deceptive. Again and again in various endeavors, in athletics, in crafts, in the arts, even in business and politics, some people are able to accomplish astonishing feats with no apparent effort. Seventy-year-olds glide down the steepest ski slopes. A potter sits at her wheel, and a beautiful bowl appears to shape itself out of the clay. A facilitator brings a fractious group into agreement simply by posing a question or two. In these instances, mind and body are aligned and everything just flows.

Left out of the picture, assumed but not mentioned in these verses, are the building of capacity and the maturation of ability. We begin with an effort and that effort matures into effortlessness. I sit straight, for instance, but if I sit rigidly, I quickly grow tired. If, however, I explore my experience in sitting straight, becoming aware of tensions in my system, I then make small adjustments. Through this process I find and connect with the natural straightness in my body. Now I sit just as straight, but with little effort or strain.

Two distinctions are important here. The first is between prescription and description — whether we interpret a teaching as a prescription for what to do or as a description of what is possible. Instruction is often interpreted as prescription. For instance, a student may be told to let his eyes rest in soft focus on a point about twelve inches in front of his nose. He looks at that point, but because he is looking at it, his eyes never rest. Alternatively, he could do nothing with his eyes when he sits, just as we do nothing with our ears. When he just lets his eyes rest, they come to rest in soft focus on that point. Then the instruction turns out to be a description of what happens with the eyes. Much of what is presented as teaching is actually descriptive, not prescriptive.

The second distinction is between method and result. Method tells us what efforts to make in practice. Result describes what those efforts lead to. Doing pushups is a method. Having strong arms is a result. Confusion on both these points is very common and is one of the reasons people may put in hours of practice to little effect.

Balance plays an important role here. If we stand on one leg, we notice immediately that the body is never static but constantly adjusting. While we are never really in balance, every adjustment is a movement in the direction of balance. With practice, we are able to stand on one leg and appear to be quite steady because our adjustments have become more subtle and precise and require less counter-compensation.

As we rest more deeply, we refine our ability to sense imbalance and to make subtle adjustments. At the same time, our response to imbalance becomes more intuitive and natural. The results of all these efforts in practice are twofold: we are able to rest in empty clarity without effort, and we are able to rest in difficult and intense experiences without disturbance. We may feel that we are doing nothing at all, but this nothing is very different from the nothing we began with.

Again, we cannot just decide to practice this way. It is something we grow into. Most of us will benefit from expert guidance along the way. In fact, most of us probably need the guidance, just as most of us need a teacher if we are going to play a musical instrument or learn to draw. The hours, days and years of work a musician spends practicing enable him or her to play even the most intricate passages without apparent effort. In the same way, the hours, days and years we put into practice mature into a practice that is free from effort.

Complete — all teachings on behavior end up in no do's or don't's.

In the same way that all paths of practice end up in no effort, all teachings on behavior end up in no do's or don't's. However, the journey from explicit ethical guidelines to no do's or don't's takes place in the richness and messiness of daily life and is often more difficult than meditation practice.

Guidelines for behavior inevitably bring us into the domain of ethics and morality, where ethics is what guides our behavior when we secede from society to pursue a practice, and morality is what guides our behavior in society. In verse 18 of the *Tao Te Ching*, Lao Tzu points out that hypocrisy arises only when learning or integrity is regarded as something special and that family values are invoked only when the institution of the family is in trouble. For

Lao Tzu, moral guidelines are not absolutes but expressions of a disconnection from the immediacy of life. They are formulated to counter imbalances, yet they generate imbalances of their own.

Gone are the days of traditional societies, at least in most parts of the world, when everyone in a given society held the same overarching worldview and understanding about right and wrong. Many people in modern societies would like to return to an absolute standard, a wish that often takes expression in various forms— the modern phenomenon of fundamentalism (religious, political, moral or economic), for example, or the claim that some truths are universal and should be adopted by everyone. In a pluralist society, we tend to rely on our own personal values. Our sense of right and wrong is frequently defined by context and perspective. Because our values define our identity, we seek to validate our stances and persuade (if not coerce) others to adopt them. Ironically, we are likely to be more dogmatic and strident in the advocacy and defense of these personal values than we are of those that are generally accepted.

Morality provides groups with cohesion—a set of shared values and priorities that determine with whom we do or do not connect. This function is also intimately connected with reputation, with what other people think of us. In the world of social interaction, and especially in the world of social media, we have to manage our reputation because it is, in effect, our personal brand. It determines to a large extent which groups we belong to and which deem us worthy of consideration, respect or membership, whatever circles we move in.

This cohesive function inevitably leads members of a given group to diminish or dismiss the values and priorities of other groups. Conflicting ideas about right and wrong and about what is true become the seeds of tension and conflict—conflicts that are resolved or fought out in the political, economic and social spheres. Hence, as the Korean monk Manhae wrote in *Everything Yearned For*:

Yes, I understand ethics, morality, law
are nothing but the smoke worshipping the sword and gold.

This function of morality with its attendant concern for belonging and reputation is in stark contrast to the ethics of Mahayana Buddhism, in which we find guidelines such as this one from *Mind Training in Eight Verses*:

> When scorn and insult become my lot,
> Expressions of some jealousy,
> I alone accept defeat
> And award the other victory.

This and similar guidelines serve a third and very different function. They support and reinforce the efforts we make in practice. To this end, they replace the external enemy with an internal enemy, our own reactivity. Victory over an external enemy is replaced by victory over the internal enemy, our ordinary reactive impulses. Ethical guidelines in this context are not about right and wrong *per se*, though they are often interpreted that way. Nor are they about the values of a group or community, though they have often been corrupted for that purpose. They are, instead, guidelines for practice, for a practice that has nothing to do with living in society but has everything to do with freeing oneself from the grip of reactive emotions and the habituated patterns developed through social interaction.

However, in the context of direct awareness, the whole notion of enemy, external or internal, has no ground. Consequently, there can be no fixed ethical or behavioral guidelines. Instead, one lives moment to moment in the open transparent knowing of mind itself.

What does a life led this way look like? My teacher's favorite pith instruction was "Just recognize and rest." When I sit and just recognize what is arising and do not do anything to or with it, a clarity arises. That clarity is not something that I can point to and say, "It is this." While it seems to be nothing at all, it is, simultaneously, a knowing. My ethical effort in life consists in living that knowing. I do not know where that knowing will lead. In the past, it has led me to some painful and dark places. In those difficulties, for better or worse, I trusted the knowing and I found a way through. Whether the outcome was through good fortune or some deeper principle at work, I do not know. Nevertheless, I have learned that when I depart from that knowing, problems arise and things can go seriously wrong.

To live that knowing is to keep moving in the direction of balance, where balance is the union of knowing and acting at the point at which experience arises. Because life is dynamic, imbalances inevitably arise and call for a response, even if the response is no action. We never are in balance, but, with practice, our movements in the direction of balance become more precise and more refined. The ethical imperative in any given situation is to move in the direction of balance. That means that, from that knowing, we respond to what arises to the best of our abilities. Obligation is not imposed from outside. It arises out of a personal choice as to where we take a stand in response to imbalance.

In this approach to life, I cannot ignore what arises or what I encounter, nor can I shut out what is inconvenient. I cannot manipulate what I experience nor control what does or does not happen. Ordinarily, what I say or do in any moment is largely shaped by emotional and biological conditioning. Like the tectonic plates that make up the surface of this planet, reactive patterns shift and move inside me in ways that I can neither control nor predict. These movements may open fissures in my personality into which I tumble out of control. They may cause massive earthquakes that shake me to my core as different patterns collide and fracture. The notion that "I" exist as a seamlessly integrated personality is a Platonic pipe dream. All I can do is meet what does arise, open, and stand there until a way is clear. There is no guarantee that things will not turn out badly in a conventional sense. When they do, I meet that situation and then the next, learning in the process how to make similar occurrences less likely.

Anything else seems arbitrary, contrived and self-serving.

If I adopt or accept a set of guidelines that tells me what to do, I am no longer living that clarity. I am just following a rulebook. Why do I choose to live this way? Perhaps Rilke said it best in *Letters to a Young Poet*:

> This most of all: ask yourself in the stillest hour of your night: must I write? Dig into yourself for a deep answer. And if this should be affirmative, if you may meet this earnest question with a strong, simple "I must," then build your life in accordance with this necessity....

Complete — the essence of result is to be free of hope.

Many people find the idea of living without hope depressing, but to live without hope is a profound freedom and peace. To let go of hope is to let go of wanting things to be different from what they are. Even in the midst of pain, tragedy or devastation, when we accept how things are without reservation, something lets go in both mind and body. Experience takes on an indescribable exquisiteness in which a profound peace, a deep quiet joy and a seemingly paradoxical sense of freedom are all present. This possibility in human experience is one of the central principles of Buddhism because it demonstrates vividly how suffering ends. It ends when we stop struggling with what arises in our experience of life. It comes to an end not by trying to change what we are experiencing but by being completely in it.

When I stop wanting things to be different from what they are, I am more able to notice and be in the actual experience of life, right now, just as it is. In other words, I am more likely to stop and smell the roses or just be with a friend. Letting go of wants and desires does not stop me from imagining. It does not stop me from creating. It does not stop me from working at writing this book. But there is a difference. The meaningfulness of an action or activity is not based in the results that I hope to achieve but in the fact that life, that is, the totality of what I am experiencing right now, is calling for this activity. The challenge is to find the balance in all the different pushes and pulls that make up our lives. For that, I have found that the best way is to open to everything that is calling to me in my life — everything — whether it seems to be important or not. I do not try to sort out the flood of desires, demands, challenges, hopes, fears, aversions, longings and ideals. I just sit in the whole mess, until the direction and the next step become clear.

Dante had it wrong. *Abandon all hope, ye who enter here* leads to awakening, not to the realms of hell.

Verse 2.2

>Awakening mind is the essence of all experience.
>Awakening mind is the heart of all awakened ones.
>Awakening mind is the life force of all beings.
>Apparent and ultimate are not found in awakening mind.

Awakening mind (Skt. *bodhicitta*) is an experience of such clarity and freedom that all conceptual interpretations of experience fall by the wayside. This groundless clarity takes expression in a heartfelt yearning that others know the same freedom. These two, the groundless clarity and the heartfelt yearning, do not stand in opposition to each other. They are experienced together.

To describe awakening mind, to communicate how he experiences it, Jigmé Lingpa makes use of another framework used in the Tibetan tradition — essence, nature and function. What is it? How is it? What does it do?

Awakening mind is the essence of all experience.

What is awakening mind? In Idries Shah's *The Book of the Book* there is a short tale in which one person says, "When you realize the difference between the container and the content, you will have knowledge." What is the container for human experience? When I ask myself that question, everything stops. In that stopping, I experience awakening mind. The question puts me in touch with experience itself. A space opens up, a space that I would be hard put to describe, but that space can contain anything that I could conceivably experience.

Awakening mind is the heart of all awakened ones.

How is awakening mind? The nature of awakening mind is compassion. As Jamgön Kongtrul writes at the beginning of *The Great Path of Awakening*, "Even when you attain buddhahood, there is nothing to do but work for the welfare of beings with nonreferential compassion." Compassion, the heartfelt yearning that others not suffer, is the core of the whole enterprise. The more we know the groundlessness of experience, the more we see that it is not necessary to struggle with what we experience. That understanding takes expression as compassion, not as a felt sentiment but as how we live our lives.

Awakening mind is the life force of all beings.

What does awakening mind do? For Jigmé Lingpa, awakening mind, this empty clarity that manifests as compassion, is what animates all beings. This is probably the one article of faith in Buddhism: in the end, we do take care of each other. Numerous philosophers and theologians, biologists and neuroscientists, psychologists and sociologists have sought to prove through the logic of their respective disciplines that, despite the atrocities of which humanity is all too capable, our being is fundamentally based in compassion. Such proofs are inherently problematic. They seek to imprison human experience in the straightjacket of ontological certainty.

Human experience is too varied, too diverse. More moving and inspiring to me is how openness and compassion consistently crop up in the most unlikely places. Even John Le Carré, as disillusioned an author as one is likely to find, makes the same point in *The Secret Pilgrim* when he puts these words into the mouth of George Smiley at his retirement from the British Secret Service: "If you allow this institution, or any other, to steal your compassion away, wait, and see what you become." Absent compassion we cease to be human.

Apparent and ultimate are not found in awakening mind.

On the one hand, when we see through the confusion of our own mind, we know directly the groundlessness of experience. On the other, we are awed by the fullness of experience. There is no way to put words to this seeming dichotomy. This is just how life is. These two aspects of awakening mind, in the hands of both practitioners and philosophers, evolved (and eventually calcified) into the conceptual framework called *the two truths*: what is ultimately true and what is apparently true (often translated as *absolute truth* and *relative truth*). Jigmé Lingpa, however, is not seduced by such conceptual formulations. In this line he points out that in the actual experience of awakening mind, ideas such as apparent and ultimate truth do not arise at all. They are conceptual designations, nothing more.

Verse 2.3

> To say "it is not" does not make it empty.
> To maintain "it is" does not make it solid.
> It is a realm beyond thought — untroubled, nothing held, nothing dispelled —
> A space free from the complications of thought and object.

We cannot make something into what it already is. As a Navajo proverb says, "You cannot wake up a person who is pretending to sleep."

When we fall into a profound experience of groundlessness, we are inclined to say, "There is nothing there." The phrase "there is nothing there" normally makes sense as a statement when we are pointing to an empty cupboard, say. When we are talking about our experience of mind or of life, the word "nothing" does not represent a fact. In that moment, our experience of life could hardly be fuller, more alive or awake. When we say of our experience of mind, "There is nothing there," we do not use the same tone of voice as when we are making a statement about a cupboard. Our voice is probably softer and imbued with awe and wonder. The words are alive as we say them, and the experience we are describing comes alive in others.

In the same way, when the extraordinary clarity and vividness of this groundless knowing leaves us astonished and amazed, we might say, "It's just there!" In doing so, we are not stating a fact: we are describing our experience. We are not making anything into anything, and if someone asked us, "What is there?" we would be hard put to answer.

The experience of awakening mind, groundless and vivid, is beyond words, beyond description, beyond conceptualization. In comparison, intellectual understanding is like quicksand — it sucks us in and the more we struggle to understand, the deeper we sink into conceptual thinking.

"To enter the unknown, you need a method, and then you use that method very precisely." These words come from an art teacher in Europe. While she was talking about the creative process, what she says applies in this context, too. We need a method, a very precise method, that brings us right into what we are experiencing without confining, reducing or restricting it, in such a way that we neither hold on to nor try to dispel what arises.

That method comes down to what Suzuki Roshi said about Soto Zen practice: absolute confidence in our fundamental nature. Like Jigmé Lingpa, Suzuki Roshi is not making a philosophical statement about the existence of a fundamental nature. Rather, he using poetic language — absolute confidence, fundamental nature — to describe how to practice. The confidence comes from knowing itself, and we just go with it. We do this without a thought about anything else. The fundamental nature is that it is turtles all the way down. We do it again and again and again, plumbing the depths, until we know in our own experience what Jigmé Lingpa is pointing to.

Verse 2.4

Because I am free from the thinking that distorts experience,
The evolution of good and evil ends completely.
What are deities, mantras and absorptions meant to do?
I am not a wakefulness that comes from practice.
My nature is universal presence:
How can seeing come through paths and levels?

In these three couplets, Jigmé Lingpa makes it clear that the wakefulness of great completion practice does not come about through a process of evolution, a directed intention or a gradual unfolding. It is just there.

Because I am free from the thinking that distorts experience,
The evolution of good and evil ends completely.

In the first couplet he is talking about karma. Karma is a description of how thoughts, words and actions evolve into experienced results. The idea that buddhas or bodhisattvas are somehow free of karma led to theological questions that Buddhists have debated for thousands of years. The Zen tradition sees this as such an important matter that it is the crux of the second koan in *The Gateless Gate*, the koan *Hyakujō and a Fox*.

One of the key exchanges in this koan takes place between Hyakujō and a mysterious man who attends his talks. One day Hyakujō asks the man who he is and where he comes from. The old man replies, "I used to be the abbot of this monastery, but I have been reborn as a fox five hundred times because I said that a buddha is free of karma. Please enlighten me on this matter." Hyakujō replies, "A buddha is one with karma." On hearing these words, the old man is enlightened.

To claim that one is free of karma is equivalent to the claim that one is free of gravity. No one is free of gravity, not even in intergalactic space. On this planet, no matter who you are, if you step off a building without a parachute, you are going to hit the ground and hit it hard. In the same way, as long as we are in this world, our thoughts, words and actions shape how we experience life, no matter who we are or what we may have experienced.

Karma is a way earlier cultures described the process of growth and evolution of patterns of behavior. They also relied on the idea of karma to explain why good things sometimes happened to bad people and bad things happened to good people, explanations that served to give order and meaning to a world that they could not otherwise understand.

Karma is not a magical force and it is not cause and effect, at least not in the way these terms are usually understood. In the West, a cause is something that acts on something else to produce a result. A virus, for instance, acts on the human organism to produce a disease. My own teacher explained karma by using the metaphor of a seed growing into a tree and bearing fruit. In everyday English, we would not say that an acorn causes an oak tree. However, if we plant an acorn, the acorn becomes a sprout, then a shoot, then a sapling and eventually matures into an oak tree — and it produces acorns, not apples. In the same way, our thoughts, words and actions grow into how we experience our lives. A more contemporary metaphor might be evolution in complex adaptive systems, but the point remains the same: thoughts, words and actions evolve into patterns of thinking and acting that shape how we experience the world and predispose (but do not determine) how we are likely to act.

What, then, are we to make of Jigmé Lingpa's statement "The evolution of good and evil ends completely"?

One of the turning points in *Hyakujō and a Fox* is when Hyakujō says, *A buddha is one with karma.* This statement means that when we are awake and present, we live precisely in balance with the dynamics and processes that shape the world in which we live. To be one with karma is to know and respond to the different pulls and pushes we experience in our lives, moment to moment. It is an intimate dance with what is and has nothing to do with transcending or ignoring what we experience.

As human beings, we constantly want things to be different from what they are. We attempt to control, manipulate or ignore whatever we find problematic. This oppositional stance constantly reinforces our sense of being an entity that is different from or separate from the world. We like what pleases us, we dislike what threatens us and we are not concerned with the rest. From there, it is a short step to the development of the concepts of good and evil.

When we are free of the thinking that distorts experience, the three poisons — attraction, aversion and indifference — lose their power. We let go of wanting things to be different and simply meet what arises. We do what is possible and accept what is not. The concepts of good and evil do not arise, and we experience and relate to life without prejudice or judgment.

What are deities, mantras and absorptions meant to do?
I am not a wakefulness that comes from practice.

The next two lines are about vajrayana. Generally speaking, vajrayana practice has two aspects: creation phase, which refers to creating the experience of being the deity (with mantras and meditative absorptions as part of the process), and completion phase, which refers to completing the experience of being the deity with the experience of being empty. Both are energy-transformation practices, but completion phase also includes specific high-level energy-transformation practices designed to bring about similitudes of awakening. Because one is intentionally creating and generating certain experiences, it is not uncommon for practitioners to believe that they can create or generate awakening itself. Jigmé Lingpa's aim in this couplet is to dispel this belief. Again, a Zen story comes to mind:

A monk was meditating in the monastery courtyard. When his teacher saw the monk, he asked, "What are you doing?"

"I am meditating to attain enlightenment," the monk replied.

The teacher sat down beside him, picked up a stone and started to rub it with his robe.

After several hours, the monk turned to his teacher and asked him, "What are you doing?"

"I'm polishing this stone to make a mirror," was the reply.

"You can't make a mirror by polishing a stone," said the monk.

"Nor can you attain enlightenment by meditating," said the teacher.

Jigmé Lingpa does not see wakefulness (buddha) as a state or understanding that can be conjured into experience by the power of intention or generated through energy-transformation practices. The wakefulness that Ever-present Good represents is not a product of methods aimed at control or transcendence. It is just there.

Jamgön Kongtrul, the great nineteenth century master, put it this way in *A Summary of the Key Points in Creation and Completion*:

> When the deity's form is clear, the clear appearance is your own mind.
> Acceptance that it is not clear is your own mind.
> While you want it to be clear, what works at meditation is your own mind.
> Your mind is also timeless awareness, guru and deity.
> Everything is the arising of mind, yet mind itself is not something made.
> The beauty of this key point on the two phases is how comprehensive it is:
> No matter how many different creation-phase practices you do,
> If you make awareness clear and just keep it from wandering,
> Clarity arises as clarity-emptiness and disturbance arises as
>   disturbance-emptiness.

In other words, we discover wakefulness right in our own experience, whatever we happen to be experiencing. This wakefulness is quite different from the wakefulness understood as the ability to observe thoughts and feelings coming and going without being caught by them. That wakefulness is like a person sitting on the banks of a river, watching the water tumble over rocks, swell into waves and swirl in eddies. The wakefulness Jigmé Lingpa is pointing to is more like a person in a kayak, right in the river, tumbling over rapids, gliding through pools, constantly rebalancing and resetting direction in the shifting currents, swirling eddies and swelling waves.

Great completion practice is about being awake in the thick of life, which is why it is so challenging and so intriguing. The wakefulness is already there. Practice just brings it out.

My nature is universal presence:
How can seeing come through paths and levels?

As for the third couplet about paths and levels, suppose I am in a dark room. I can just see the outlines of a few objects, but there is not enough light for me to see things clearly. I stumble around, bumping into furniture and knocking over lamps and chairs. After a while, I figure out that I have to stay still, let my eyes adjust to the darkness and then move slowly and carefully, relying on the subtle play of shadow that I can just detect at the limit of my vision. Then a light goes on. At first, I cannot see anything. All I experience is light — bright, bright light. It has no inside, no outside. There is just light. I am surprised, shocked, perhaps exhilarated, perhaps afraid. Then my eyes begin to adjust. Now everything in the room is brilliantly clear — no more vague shadows and barely discernible differentiations of murky grays and blacks. I see color, shape and form. I am also aware of the space in the room, which was always there even though I was not aware of it. It is a completely different world, yet it is the same room I have been in all along. I can see clearly now, yet my eyes have not changed. Everything is bright and full of life. Nor is there any restriction on what I can see. Because I can navigate the room so much more easily, I feel I can do anything!

Seeing is seeing. Knowing is knowing. The paths and levels mentioned in this couplet refer to the degree to which one is able to live in that knowing. They do not refer to the knowing itself. We cannot make the knowing come into being through practice. Nor does it develop through a sequence of levels. The knowing is already present and does not change.

These three couplets are descriptions, not instructions. They describe a profound shift that takes place when we stumble upon this way of experiencing life. We feel free, awake and at peace — free from groping around in the dark and bumping into things; awake because we now understand that we lived in the dark; and at peace because we know where we are, perhaps for the first time.

When this shift takes place, our understanding of good and bad changes, but that does not mean we are free from karma. We cannot walk through things and we still bump into them if we do not look where we are going. Our ability to see is not something we created or generated — our eyes are the same as they were before the light went on. Our new sight enables us to see things more clearly now, but not because we polished our glasses.

All that has happened is that, somehow, a light went on. I did not turn it on, but it happened.

It is tempting, very tempting, to universalize our experience and say, "This is how it is." We often want to tell others how it is for us, in the hope that our description will help them experience a similar shift. That is how compassion operates. But when we try to do so, words fail us. Buddha Shakyamuni had the same problem. After his awakening he did not speak to anyone for seven weeks because he could not figure out how to explain what he had experienced.

Explanations are usually counterproductive. They rely on the conceptual mind, an ineffective method when it comes to communicating non-conceptual experience. Further, they lead to in-groups, the ones who understand the explanation, the "awakened"—a problem that goes back to the time of the Buddha and the formation of the first council after Buddha Shakyamuni died. Ananda, who had faithfully retained all Buddha's teachings, was initially excluded from the council because he was not awakened.

Likewise, descriptions of results are rarely helpful. They may serve to inspire, but that is as far as they go. People often take these descriptions as instruction and do not understand why their practice goes nowhere. Again, this problem goes far back in history. Much of what one reads in the sutras is a description and a celebration of results: one often has to dig deep and pay close attention to find the nuggets of actual instruction.

Verse 2.5

Therefore, having loosened the knots of expectations,
Let go of outlook's razor-edge and rest.
Step out of deep practice's cozy cocoon and rest.
Break out of behavior's constricting conventions and rest.
Throw away expectations for dramatic results and rest.

Up to this point Jigmé Lingpa has been describing the ground, the basis for practice. Now he talks about practice itself, the refinement of the fine art of doing nothing—nothing whatsoever.

When I began meditation practice many years ago, I had high expectations, but when it came to meditation on the breath, I was far too wound up in both mind and body to sit still for even a few minutes. I did not even see what resting with the breath would accomplish. My unrealistic hopes of deep meditation experience were soon dashed to pieces, and I ran straight into my greatest fear—the extraordinary awareness about which I had read would forever be inaccessible to me. I gave up on sitting meditation and asked my teacher to give me something I could do. I had heard about the practice of prostrations and thought that that practice might be a possibility. Initially, he was reluctant, but in the face of my repeated requests, he eventually said, "Okay, do a hundred thousand prostrations." That was something I could do and I did. In the end, I had to do a hundred thousand prostrations several times before I could even begin to rest in meditation.

In the three-year retreat, when we started mahamudra practice, the practice of direct awareness in the Shangpa and Kagyu traditions, it soon became clear to me that effective practice depended on an ability to rest, to rest deeply. Again, my hopes and fears took over. I could not tolerate the physical and emotional discomfort I encountered every day in sitting. Unable to rest, I soon became tangled up in knots. It was more than frustrating. Any movement I made pulled the knots tighter. Whenever I thought I had undone one knot, I found that I had just tied several more. What to do? I had no idea which way to turn — probably just as well in the circumstances, as the knots were so tight that I could not turn anyway.

Learning how to do nothing did not come easily.

As for *outlook's razor edge*, outlook has always made sense to me. It points directly to the groundlessness of experience. It cuts through projections and confusion of all kinds. Even when I was very upset or disturbed, if I stopped and looked, or just asked the question, "What is this?" I always experienced a shift: a space opened up and something let go. Whatever I was experiencing, no matter how painful or confusing, how intense or banal or how uncomfortable or pleasant, it would be revealed as just an experience that comes and goes. Outlook was like a razor that cut through the solidity of my own projections, and that was a relief.

Here Jigmé Lingpa says to forget about employing outlook in this or any other way. Just rest, he says. For me, this instruction presents a challenge. If I just rest and let go of cutting, I cannot use outlook to open up a space in which to rest. Instead, I have to rest in exactly what I am experiencing right now.

As for *practice's cozy cocoon*, I have certainly worked with students who related to practice this way, particularly people who have trained in the *jhanas* (a set of practices in the Theravadan tradition in which one trains in four well-defined levels of attention). I have less ability here, but there is still a certain appeal to resting deeply. Mind and body are refreshed in a way that a nap or even a good night's sleep does not do. After many years of struggle and difficulty, I now enjoy the experience of resting deeply in practice. Why not? The experience is usually quite pleasant, if not blissful, and you have the satisfaction of feeling that you are meditating deeply. But meditation can be a cozy cocoon. So can the whole practice environment. Again, Jigmé Lingpa says to let go of any inclination to seek comfort, peace or anything else through practice. I can grow too comfortable, and that is when I need to interrupt my "deep meditation," forget about it and just be there.

With respect to behavior, there are many ethical guidelines associated with every practice. These guidelines are not about right and wrong in the moral sense, but about what does and does not support practice. All too easily, the supportive intent of the ethical guidelines can be overlooked, and they then become a list of do's and don't's. Because they are so intricately woven into the fabric of practice and teaching, even if we do not pay much attention to them, they still become part of our thinking. We end up feeling obliged or constrained for no apparent reason other than feeling that this is the "right" or "wrong" way to act.

It is not so easy to break out of these constricting conventions. Simply to do the opposite to what feels like an obligation or constraint does not work because the opposite of a reaction is still a reaction.

For instance, a persistent pattern in my behavior is to conform to expectations, whether from inside (coming from the practices I aspire to) or from outside (socially responsible behavior). Over time I noticed that the constant effort to conform to these expectations led to subtle forms of suppression. While I generally became less reactive and more responsive to others, my efforts ended up numbing me deep inside. At my core, I became an emotional iceberg. While I am unlikely to be completely free of that conforming habit of mine, when I notice it running now, I drop any notion of "right conduct" or "right action" and just rest in the experience of the pattern: the physical sensations associated with both conforming and rebelling; emotional reactions such as fear, anger or judgment; and all the stories about what might or might not happen as a consequence of my actions. When I can rest in the whole mess (and the mess includes all the sensations of the emotional iceberg as well as the uncertainty and fear of responding openly from the groundlessness of experience), and be clear and at peace at the same time, then other possibilities open up, possibilities that are not restricted to the conventions of practice or society or rebellion against them.

The descriptions of sublime results in the sutras and tantras are presented in beautiful and magnificent poetry, but I find it difficult to relate to them in my own experience, even when I regard them as metaphor. At this point I am not sure what the result of practice is or what it is meant to be. I have the impression, both from my own experience and from conversations with more experienced friends and colleagues, that the result becomes less and less well-defined as one's experience in practice evolves. Yet, whenever I read Jigmé Lingpa's poem or similar writings by other great teachers, I am continually struck by their descriptions of ways to correct even subtle imbalances and how these descriptions act as a reliable guide to moving deeper into the mystery of experience.

I still live with expectations, even though I am not sure what they are about. When I become aware that they have caught me once again, the only thing for me to do is to let go of any sense of achievement and any hope for a dramatic result, and just be in the experience of what is happening right now.

Verses 2.6 and 2.7

> Practice or not practice — attention goes beyond.
> Act or not act — decisions melt away.
> Empty or not empty — awakening mind is beyond.
> Be or not be — there is a vastness wherein
> These differences fade away.
>
> Awareness — not a word, not a thought, no description at all —
> Has as its axis no corrective, no holding a position.
> Its nature is bare, steady, fresh and unfolding,
> A vastness free from all effort and complications.
> Rest where there is no change or time.

In these two verses, Jigmé Lingpa eloquently describes just how radical great completion practice is. A Nasrudin story comes to mind.

On this occasion, Nasrudin is a magistrate. A man dressed only in his underwear enters Nasrudin's courtroom. He explains that he is a tourist and complains that someone in the village has stolen his clothes. He demands that Nasrudin have the village searched to find the miscreant, arrest him and return the stolen clothing. Nasrudin looks at him carefully and then asks, "You are still wearing your underwear, aren't you?"

"Of course," says the tourist.

"Well," says Nasrudin, "it wasn't someone from our village. We do things thoroughly around here."

The first verse here is all about letting go, letting go completely. If we are going to do this, says Jigmé Lingpa, we do it thoroughly. We take the underwear, too.

Forget about practicing. And forget about not practicing. (Note what happens when you read these two sentences.) Decisions and judgments reverberate, of course, but the reverberations fade away if we do not dwell on what we should do or what we think.

What is emptiness? What is empty? What is not empty? We do not need to engage these questions. They do not go anywhere. An instruction from *Mind Training in Seven Points* covers this — *let even the remedy release naturally*. Poof! We come back.

Other ideas come, too. Do I exist? Do I not exist? There is no need to engage any debate, analysis or speculation. All of that can be left to the philosophers, the psychologists and the neuroscientists. We just rest in the space in which these questions arise. If we do not feed them, they fall away, too.

What is left is a particular kind of awareness, a knowing that cannot be understood or described, a knowing to which no correction or adjustment can be applied. If we do not do anything with it or to it (and that is the hard part), it is there, Spartan in its simplicity, constant in its presence, vivid and awake, revealing and refreshing itself moment to moment. It seems both extraordinary and absurd that anything could be so simple, so effortless, so wonderful and so immediately at hand — right under our noses, so to speak. We just have to shake our head at how obvious all this is when we happen upon it.

Here there is a peace and a freedom that seems to stand outside of time, a freedom to which change and time seem not to apply. It goes beyond anything in our ordinary lives. People have built whole philosophies out of it, others worship it and still others ritualize the practices associated with it — all to no end. The point is to know it — nothing more, nothing less. To do that, we have to let everything go. It is turtles again, all the way down.

Elimination of errors

Where the second section set out the central theme of natural freedom, the third section provides more explicit instructions on how to bring out the experience of this freedom. In particular, Jigmé Lingpa points out a number of subtle errors — ways that we slip from doing nothing into doing something.

The first six verses follow the framework of outlook, practice and behavior, a framework that Jigmé Lingpa used at the beginning of section 2. The first two verses describe errors in outlook: on the one hand, not trusting that the possibility of being awake is present in us, and, on the other, reifying or concretizing that possibility. The next two verses focus on errors in practice: either trying to make something happen or trying to stop anything from happening. The third pair describes two persistent errors in behavior: the tendency to track the content of experience and the tendency to try to control what we experience.

In the second part, Jigmé Lingpa returns to the theme of resting and doing nothing at a deeper level still. The first three verses are a gradual crescendo, beginning with the reminder that the notion of practice is itself artificial. The crescendo peaks in the third verse, which for me is the heart of the whole poem:

Don't look at what arises: be what knows the arising.
Like an oak peg in hard ground,
Stand firm in awareness that knows,
And go deep into the mystery.

The next verse is a short dénouement, warning how it is still possible to go astray if we fall into any kind of conceptualization. Then he launches into the finale, shifting gradually from instruction and method to a climactic description of result — what it is like to know the timeless freedom of simple presence.

Verse 3.1

Wonder of wonders!

Thus, awakening mind, in which there is nothing to give up or attain,
This buddha nature, which is awareness and peace,
Is present in you. Still, it is trapped in a cage of inventions.
Any notion of practice clouds the heart of the matter.

In this verse, the instruction is in the last line: any notion of practice clouds or distorts the heart of the matter. The heart of the matter is buddha nature, of course — the potential for direct awareness, peace and freedom that is present in all experience.

While the premise that all beings have the potential to be awake is largely accepted in Mahayana Buddhism, it is easy to develop an abstract idea of buddha nature as something that is present in all beings. That interpretation has repeatedly provoked a refutation of buddha nature, on the grounds that it implies a self, a soul or other kind of entity that negates the notion of non-self. "Mahayana essentialist!" is an epithet that has been hurled at me on more than one occasion. Such problems arise only because a poetic expression has been taken literally, and both those who use the term and those who criticize it have lost touch with the experience that the original expression is pointing to. Buddha nature, though it has evolved into a philosophical or theological concept, refers, first and foremost, to an experience.

The compiler of *The Gateless Gate* deemed this point so important that he placed *Zhaozhou's Dog* first in that collection. Zhaozhou was once asked if a dog has buddha nature. "Wu!" he replied, where *wu* is the Chinese syllable that indicates negation (often rendered as *mu*, the Japanese equivalent). Ever since, Zhaozhou's negation has echoed down the corridors of time. The koan calls on the student to demonstrate his or her understanding of buddha nature, the possibility of being awake and present in any experience, without resorting to doctrine or belief.

Instead of positing a potential for awakening (a position that all too easily leads to the rigidity of belief), I start with my experience right now, what I am feeling, what I am sensing and what I am thinking—and just sit. I sit because there is a longing in my heart. Whether I call that a longing for freedom, for peace or for knowing, it does not matter. It is there. I can try to put it into words, but the words always fall short.

The longing is often paradoxical. It may take us to places that we would not necessarily choose to go. One person wrote to me and described how her longing took her to a place of pain, a pain that she had not known was there. She did not understand it, but it seemed to want to be felt. Her practice became about feeling that pain, even if that meant only a little bit each day. Gradually, she was able to feel more and more of it. Despite the intensity she continued to follow her yearning. Then, much to her surprise, she found that she felt both more complete and more at peace right in the experience of the pain. After that, the pain ceased to be an issue. Others have told me that they discovered a peace or a freedom that was different from anything they could have imagined and from anything they could have deserved. Where this longing takes us may be radically different from where we think we should be going, where we want to be going or how we are used to being.

If we have any notion of practice, we inevitably have an agenda: this is what I am going to do and this is what is meant to happen. Any such agenda prevents us from letting that longing resolve itself in its own time and in it its own way. Its resolution may be no resolution, but that is still its resolution.

These reflections take us back to the box, of course, though here Jigmé Lingpa calls it *a cage of inventions*. As long as our agenda is to find a way out of the box, we remain stuck in it.

Quite often I notice that I have been following a train of thought, thinking about something. When that recognition happens, I come back. If the distraction is insistent, it is usually because I am not feeling something in my body. I reconnect with my body and there it is—something that I did not want to feel. When I experience a deepening peace and clarity, hope often springs up, hope for some kind of insight or transcendent experience. I now know those hopes are just thoughts, and they no longer have the power they once had.

The same holds for fear, the fear that all my efforts are pointless. Sometimes I experience nothing special at all. Sometimes my body is so uncomfortable that it is difficult to sit for the whole period. Even so, I do not think in terms of good days or bad days, just "that's what happened today."

How is it possible to practice this way? Recall Suzuki Roshi's words: "Absolute confidence in our fundamental nature." When I say these words to myself, my body straightens. A strength and a determination arise that seem to come from inside, but I do not really know where they come from. My mind clears and I have a direction, though it is hard to put that direction into words. Do the clarity and direction come from buddha nature? Where do they lead? Wu! I have no idea. The heart has its longings, and this way of practicing is a response. The rest is not my business.

Verse 3.2

> No origin, nothing there: that's just how it is.
> Perception doesn't arise or vanish.
> When you make it more than that,
> It's like making form out of what is formless:
> You lose touch with what is natural. How reactive you become!

There is something wonderfully tenacious about the human proclivity to name an experience and then make an object out of the name. An academic word for this tendency is *reification*, but the proclivity has been known since ancient times. The opening lines of the *Tao Te Ching* point out how this propensity is problematic in the context of spiritual practice:

> A way that becomes the way is not the way.
> A name that becomes the name is not the name.

When we are present, deeply present, in what we experience, it is turtles all the way down. Experience is groundless. When we look into that fathomless depth, we often recoil with fear. We feel as if we are jumping off a cliff into a bottomless abyss. Yet, there is nothing to fear. Because there is no bottom, there is no end to our fall. It is turtles all the way down and we can fall forever.

Again, when we are deeply present, there is at the same time a nothing-there quality. The nothing-there quality can be likened to the space in a room. Yet, even though we say, "There is nothing there," we are still aware. We know, but we cannot put any words to this knowing. The knowing can be likened to the light in a room. We cannot say where the light comes from or what it is made of, any more than we can say where the space comes from or what it is made of. Beginning and end have no meaning when applied to the space and the light. They are just there, and that is how it is.

In that empty knowing, perception happens. Jigmé Lingpa writes *Perception doesn't arise or vanish*. He is not saying that there is no perception. There is, but it does not start or stop. It is just there and then not there, whether the perception is of a thought, a feeling or a sensation.

It is a very different way of experiencing our lives. Nevertheless, we find that we can function, though not exactly as before. We now know that the content of experience is not solid, ultimate or determined. Thoughts, feelings and sensations just come and go. It seems that they come from nowhere and go nowhere, and they do not have the same hold on us as they did before. In particular, we come to know that we do not have to react to them.

Nevertheless, many of us find it difficult to relate to a way of experiencing life in which everything is simultaneously so vivid and so ephemeral. A part of us grasps for something to hold on to, an anchor, even if all we do is make this experience something special, give it a name and make it into some thing. Then we at least have a direction, if not a goal, by which to orient ourselves.

Now we enter a carrot-and-donkey situation. We take a step toward the carrot and that movement starts us on a path. We take more steps, but the carrot is somehow still out of reach. We keep taking steps. We build up strength, stamina and abilities; we learn methods and skills, but the carrot is still in front of us, and we seem to be no nearer than when we started. Sometimes we think that if we just understood the goal better, if we just understood this concept that we ourselves have made up, we would be able to reach our goal. The more we try to understand it, however, the more we tie ourselves up in concepts. Frustrated, confused and exhausted, we completely lose touch with what is natural. We become more and more desperate and more and more reactive.

It is hard to let go of words and concepts. It is hard to let go of ideas. When we consciously try to let go of an idea, it imprisons us. For example, I might say to you, "Don't think of an elephant." Now, how do you get rid of the elephant?

In this context, then, how do we practice an outlook in which there is nothing to hold on to without being trapped by our own words and ideas?

It all comes down to this: as soon as I recognize that I am engaged in thinking, I have already returned. Now all I need to do is rest right there. Some people find that pausing for a breath helps to break the momentum of the train of thinking. Others find that focusing on the breath is more of an interruption. The key point is just to recognize and rest.

In the same way, as soon as I recognize that I am explaining or describing to myself what I am experiencing, I rest.

When I become aware of that I am hoping, fearing or dreading, I return and rest.

If I think that I see, understand, feel or know something, I return and rest.

Whenever I notice that I am bored, elated, depressed or flooded with feelings of well-being, I return and rest.

And if I find that I am wondering about where all this is going, I return and rest.

Verse 3.3

> Some people cut off the ebb and flow of thoughts and feelings
> And construct an emptiness practice contaminated by goal-seeking.
> Their forced and constricted practice wears them out.
> Serious problems develop when reactive energy enters the life channel.

In the three-year retreat, it did not take long for me to appreciate that one of the essential abilities for mahamudra practice is the ability to rest. My inability to rest physically, emotionally or mentally gave rise to serious problems.

The tension in my body eventually made me quite ill. By the end of my second retreat, it was clear to me that there was no possibility of my continuing into a third. There was nothing wrong with me from a conventional medical point of view, yet I was quite weak, had little stamina, seriously depressed and pretty shaky emotionally. While the illness took physical form, it was not physically based—a fact that I was more than a little resistant to accepting. I had had dreams during the retreat that indicated it was a karmic illness, a category of illness in the Tibetan tradition that cannot be cured by conventional treatments. Other dreams indicated a karmic block—again, a kind of block that is not amenable to treatment, not even ritual treatment. Nevertheless, after the retreat I continued to look for treatments. I tried every conceivable modality, all to no avail.

Focused attention raises the level of energy in one's system, even in as simple a practice as resting in the experiencing of breathing. Practices such as loving kindness in the Theravadan tradition or devotion in the Vajrayana tradition raise energy to higher levels, allowing one to develop the higher levels of attention needed for insight. In the Tibetan tradition, deity practice, mantra recitation, and practices such as *tumo* or inner heat, lucid dreaming and sheer clarity, explicitly transform energy in the body to raise energy to still higher levels. The higher levels of energy result in increased clarity and stability in attention, but inevitably bring one into contact with deeper layers of emotional reactivity. Emotional reactivity trapped in the body can block the free circulation of energy. One effect of such blocks is that energy flows into and reinforces basic reactive patterns—survival, reproduction, or identity. These patterns often give rise to an obsession with wealth, sex, or power, respectively. Another possible effect is that energy stagnates at the block and undermines the body and organs in the vicinity. In retrospect, one way to understand the difficulties I experienced is that they were due to the stagnation of energy.

In general, long-standing energy imbalances are not amenable to medical treatment, though acupuncture, shiatsu or other energy-healing methodologies may sometimes help. The only effective way I know to work with them is to lead attention repeatedly through the block, making a consistent and careful effort over a long period of time. The energy of attention moving through the block gradually leads to the breaking up of the block. The emotional material that was trapped there is released and experienced, and energy is then able to circulate freely. Only then can one engage higher levels of attention without problem.

After the three-year retreats, I was fortunate to form a friendship with a person who knew a lot about energy and how to work with imbalances. Qi gong, tai chi, yoga and other systems all contain methods for working with imbalances but one really has to learn them from someone who understands how they work. I learned balancing practices and tai chi from my friend and practiced them consistently. Slowly, over many years, my condition improved. Even so, I have never been able to return to the powerful energy-transformation practices in the Tibetan tradition and have had to find my own path. I have now identified the emotional blocks that prevented me from understanding the messages that my body was giving me in the three-year retreats and also what prevented me from understanding or doing anything about them. Because I was so focused on achieving my own idea of awakening, I kept trying to make my experience conform to my expectations—a forced and constricted practice, to use Jigmé Lingpa's words.

Resting is important. In the context of great completion practice, resting is not just physical resting. It includes letting the heart rest—letting ourselves feel all the different emotions surging within us and not try to resolve them. Resting includes letting our minds rest, too—letting the stream of thoughts and stories play itself out. There are still deeper levels of resting, and one of the purposes of many energy-transformation practices is to make it possible for us to rest even more deeply. Resting helps to create the conditions in which emotional reactivity can resolve itself—leading to a refinement of energy in the whole system. It also allows energy channels to open so that energy can circulate smoothly. And it makes it possible for us to listen to our whole system and sense imbalances before they become serious problems.

Two of my teachers, Kalu Rinpoche and Nyoshul Khenpo Rinpoche, took considerable pains to impress on me that, in Nyoshul Khenpo's words, "Mahamudra and dzogchen are two names for the same person." One day, I asked Kalu Rinpoche for instruction in great completion practice. In the three-year retreat, we had practiced several approaches to mahamudra, but nothing from dzogchen, and I thought I might be missing something. He had on his table a stack of papers, short texts with pith instructions from various teachers and traditions. He read one, a mahamudra instruction, and said, "Hmmm. Sounds like dzogchen to me." Then he read another, from a dzogchen teacher. "Hmmm," he said, "that sounds like mahamudra to me." After three or four pages the message was clear: any distinction between mahamudra and dzogchen was in my own mind. All of the instructions, one way or another, came down to "Rest, and do nothing at all." But he wanted to drive the point home. He continued to read one instruction after the other to me for over an hour and stopped only when he had finished the whole stack.

Their message has stayed with me. Nevertheless, there is a difference in emphasis between these two practices. In mahamudra, the emphasis is on no distraction. In dzogchen, the emphasis is on relaxing and opening. Relaxation and no distraction are both essential, but part of the difference in flavor between the two is this difference in emphasis. Thus, in dzogchen resting is, if anything, more important, and an inability to rest is even more of a problem.

Is resting the key to everything? Probably not. While there are important principles that apply in most situations, each person needs to find the appropriate way to apply those principles. For some, their path lies in learning how to develop and focus attention. For others, it lies in discovering how to relax and open. Some people need to learn how to stand in the face of their patterns and cut through them. Others need to learn how to let things unfold on their own. After decades of teaching and working with students from different backgrounds and with different capabilities, I feel that there is no one right way for everyone: each person must find his or her own path of practice.

Verse 3.4

> Some just do not see what is naturally present.
> Misled by what is said about presence, their practice is ineffective.
> They take as the essence of practice a dullness
> That suppresses thoughts and feelings. They are very confused.

In 2001, I moved into a new office. My assistant picked up a small painting and asked, "Where do you want to put this?"

She was holding a small minimalist piece given to me by the artist. He had applied black paint with a green tinge uniformly to the canvas, but had left bare a small patch of canvas on the bottom edge.

"Right above your desk. It will be perfect there. It's a good meditation test."

I explained to her that students would look at the painting but not see it because they were not able to see nothing. When they actually saw the painting, it was a sign that they could now look at and see nothing.

"That's crazy," she said, shaking her head in disbelief.

Three years later, a regular student stopped at her desk and asked, "When did you get that painting? It's new, isn't it?"

"I don't believe it!" my assistant said, smiling and laughing. The student was a bit disconcerted and looked to me for explanation. I smiled, too, and let her explain to the student that the painting had been there for three years.

"I don't believe it," he said. "I haven't seen it before."

It is one thing to look at nothing. It is another to see nothing. To do so, one has to be open in a certain way.

Pointing-out instructions play a key role in both mahamudra and great completion practice. A teacher, through what he or she says or does, directs the attention of the student to mind itself, this empty clear knowing that is the essence of direct-awareness practice. Sometimes the question is as simple as "How is your mind?" Sometimes it is more involved, such as "What is the difference between the mind that moves and the mind that rests?" Sometimes the question seems to make no sense at all.

My teacher invariably would find some way to give pointing-out instruction to anyone who came to see him. At first, I could not figure out what he was doing. During meetings with students, he would ask certain questions that seemed to have little to do with what the student wanted to talk about. I would translate the questions and answers as best I could. Gradually, I came to appreciate that he was giving pointing-out instructions. Most of the time his efforts went nowhere, but now and then the conversation became alive in a strange way. Though I was translating, I was not really part of the conversation. My teacher and the person present were communicating at another level.

We need to be ready for pointing-out instructions. If not, we end up looking at nothing but do not see nothing. Instead, we do not see anything and fall into a kind of dullness, a dullness that we then take as a basis for meditation. Because we are unable to describe our experience, we may understand this dullness as "inexpressible and inconceivable," but there is no vitality, no power in it. Thoughts and feelings are just dulled, as if they were experienced in a fog. Because they do not disturb us, we think our practice is in good shape. People who are prone to depression easily fall into this state, a dull stasis that goes nowhere except to a gradually increasing torpor and immobility. This state of mind is often called groundhog meditation because, like a groundhog that sleeps through the winter, one can rest in this dull state for long periods of time. Every text on direct-awareness practice includes warnings about it.

When we regard non-thought as the essence of practice, we may fall into a subtler form of dullness. It is possible to use higher levels of attention and higher levels of energy to ride above thoughts and feelings. Even though we experience bliss, clarity or non-thought or other special states, we are actually in a kind of trance and have lost touch with the clarity of natural presence. This is another instance of meditation's cozy cocoon. To step out of it, we look at what experiences the bliss, the clarity or the non-thought.

Whatever the form of dullness, there is still a wakefulness in it. When we look at nothing and we have no sense of seeing, then we look at what experiences nothing. As Mipham writes in *A Light in the Dark*:

Now, as you experience this vague knowing in which there is no thought or movement, look at what knows that this is happening, look at what is mentally or emotionally inert, and rest there.

If we do this, there comes a day when we do see nothing, and everything changes.

Verse 3.5

Some who know that movement and memory are mind
Mull over the traces as thoughts and feelings ebb and flow:
They track the arising and fading of thinking. With this meditation,
Even if they practice for a hundred years, they just spin in confusion.

Do nothing. That seems to be what Jigmé Lingpa keeps saying in different ways. Here he identifies another tendency that pulls us away from doing nothing, a tendency that reflects our insatiable need for engagement of one sort or another.

Do you remember Ajahn Chah's chair in the center of the room—just sitting there and seeing who comes to visit? Some people keep a guest book. They are unable to let the visitors just come and go. Instead, they look at their visitors' signatures and savor what happened while they were there. They keep track of the visits, mulling over what causes one to come and another to go. At best they forget that the guest book is itself a visitor. At worst, they deliberately ignore that fact and indulge their need for engagement.

Even when we know and are able to experience thought and feeling as the movement of mind, we find ways to give certain visitors a privileged status. I do the same, even when I go to the ocean and watch the waves roll in. While some break on the beach and others crash against rocks, I find myself noting bigger and smaller waves, which directions the different sets come from, how they combine to become bigger and more powerful, or how they cancel each other out, leaving the ocean almost calm for a few minutes. When I am caught up in the particulars of a wave or a set of waves, I lose the experience of the ocean—the deep underlying rumble of the surf, the long sibilants of rolling waves, the roar of the break itself as water tumbles on water, the regular crashes and the unexpected ones, the sand and rocks grating against each other, the intermittent peeps and cheeps of different birds, the gusts and buffets of the wind. I lose all of that when I follow particular waves and compare them with each other.

This verse is about not letting go of the tendency to track experience, however subtly. To track experience is to observe it, and to observe it is to be separate from it. From the perspective of great completion, as long as we track experience, we will spin in confusion and never know the clarity of natural presence.

Verse 3.6

In general, work and effort by themselves create opposition.
If you practice, you stir up all sorts of pains and discomforts.
If you don't practice, you don't see what you are and wander in confusion.
In either case, you lose touch with what is straightforward and natural.

This is Jigmé Lingpa's description of the box. While effort inevitably leads to resistance, no effort perpetuates confusion. The problem here is that we want to be the agents of our awakening, or, as Chögyam Trungpa once said, "We want to be present at our own funeral." We think that with the right balance of effort and no effort we can make something happen.

To touch what is truly straightforward and natural we have to let go of the ways of knowing that we are used to. This is no small matter. We do not let go of those ways willingly. Most of us do not even know what to let go of, let alone how. For that reason, most of us have to be pushed, tricked or tripped into letting go.

In the Mahamudra and Dzogchen traditions, pointing-out instructions are frequently given in the form of questions. The questions that a teacher asks are often interpreted as logic games, but that is not their intent. What is the color of your mind? When you picture Paris, New York or Bangkok in your mind, does your mind go to the city or does the city come to your mind? When a thought arises, what moves? When a thought goes, where does it go? These are not philosophical questions. They are intended to push us beyond our ordinary ways of knowing into direct experience. They work only if we are ready, if we have developed sufficient clarity and stability in attention to look at nothing and see. Otherwise, they come across as mind games.

In the Zen tradition, a question is put forward, and before we can say anything, the teacher may say, "If you say anything, I'll hit you. If you don't say anything, I'll hit you." Again, our ordinary way of relating to life is not able to fashion a response. The teacher's aim is to push us beyond the ordinary thinking mind, to push us to respond from our direct experience and not rely on conceptual understanding.

Another method, one that has worked throughout the centuries for many people, is the practice of devotion. Through practice and prayer, through study and service, or through some other combination of practices and activities, we form a deep emotional connection with a teacher or historical figure, someone who represents to us the possibility of being completely awake. The power of devotion — the combination of awe, respect and trust we feel in that emotional connection — enables us to let go of our usual way of relating to life. When the conditions are right, the emotional energy of faith and devotion is transformed into attention. Awareness lights up and we see — we know directly. Over the centuries, in tradition after tradition, the path of devotion has been an effective path for many. In the modern world, unfortunately, it is misunderstood, suspect and abused.

In the last line, the words *straightforward* and *natural* are used because, when we experience timeless awareness, we cannot understand how we did not see it before. We are not able to fathom why we struggled for so long with what we experience. In comparison, timeless awareness does seem straightforward and natural.

Yet, for most of us, the path to that awareness is not at all straightforward and natural. Despite the teachings that have come down through the ages, it is a trackless path. There is no trail to follow. Each of us has to find our own way. We may take a long time to recognize the pitfalls outlined in the first section. We may find it far from easy to recognize and appreciate awakening mind as Jigmé Lingpa describes it in the second section, let alone trust the practice of no practice that opens up that possibility. Even then, it takes more time and more practice to recognize the problems he describes in this section or to identify the versions of those problems we encounter in ourselves. Texts such as these are quite misleading for the average Western practitioner because we do not appreciate how condensed they are in terms of time. Each verse assumes months, if not years, of practice.

The errors that Jigmé Lingpa describes here are subtle and difficult to recognize. Only gradually do we become aware of the box we have built for ourselves, the cage of inventions. Once we recognize that box, we need determination, confidence and patience to do nothing (where even waiting counts as doing something). We have little choice in the matter, because, as Jigmé

Lingpa notes, any intentional effort or non-effort on our part puts us straight back in the box.

In the next section Jigmé Lingpa continues his instruction, but he places this verse here for a definite reason. We cannot make use of what he presents next unless we have utterly and completely exhausted our habituated approaches to practice and to knowing.

Verse 3.7

Wonder of wonders!

Because these errors stop you from going beyond ordinary experience,
Be clear that the approach of practice versus not practice
Relies on an artificial distinction. Without trying to reshape it in any way,
Rest in what you experience right now.

How do we practice without feeling we are practicing? How do we not practice without feeling that we are not practicing?

By the time we reach this point, we have learned a lot: how to cultivate attention, how to bring that attention to bear on what prevents us from experiencing what arises, how to rest in the often difficult physical and emotional sensations of patterns unfolding and releasing, how to look at and see nothing, how to mix awareness and experience, and so on. Not only have we learned these skills and built this capacity of attention, these efforts have become second nature to us, as they should.

But we still have the idea of practice: there is something to do, an effort to be made. That idea lies deeply embedded in our way of thinking and puts us in a box.

One possibility is to apply again an instruction from *Mind Training in Seven Points*, namely, *let even the remedy release naturally*. The genius of this and many similar instructions is that, as our experience and abilities evolve, we discover how to apply them at deeper levels and in different ways.

We are used to thinking of practice as a remedy. It is something we work at and apply when we recognize that we are in the grip of a reactive pattern. In other words, we develop a habit of practice, of training attention and of bringing attention to patterns of reaction. Now we let even the habit of practice release itself.

In the commentary to verse 3.2, I described how to cut through the tendency to conceptualize experience. As soon as we notice any movement into conceptualization, we cut the tendency (by taking a breath, for instance, or resetting attention) and just rest. This is, essentially, the practice of *chö* (cutting, Tib. *gcod*). The same principle applies here. As soon as we feel we are practicing in any way, we stop, take a breath if necessary, and open to what we are experiencing — physically, emotionally, cognitively — *without trying to reshape it in any way.*

In the beginning, it is messy and confusing. There is a lot of second-guessing. I often end up feeling like a dog chasing its own tail, but that is just the conceptual mind going into overtime. Because I am not doing anything, the conceptual mind revs up its activity as compensation. Nevertheless, the same principle applies: when I recognize that I am chasing my own tail, I rest in exactly what I am experiencing at that moment.

This one principle seems to apply over and over again: as soon as we recognize that we are doing something or that we are lost, we stop, and start again. This is what Kalu Rinpoche taught, over and over again, with "just recognize." This approach applies to everything and, in effect, dissolves the notion of practice itself. We just keep coming back into our life.

Verse 3.8

When you give up your reactive checking,
Managing and goal-seeking — all of it —
There is a direct knowing, open and free.
Stop changing or altering it. Rest right there.

It is all very well to say, "Stop checking or tracking your experience. Stop managing it. Stop your goal-seeking." Personally I find it hard to give up those tendencies. They are deeply ingrained. Maybe some people can let these tendencies go through an act of will. Any attempt on my part to exert such an act of will just puts me back in the box.

There is an old joke about fish. One fish asks another fish, "How's the water?" The other fish replies, "What's water?" Like the fish, we swim in water. The water we swim in is an absolutely clear awareness. We do not notice it, we do not recognize it and we do not appreciate it.

Mind is often likened to a glass of turbid water. The water becomes clear when it is left undisturbed and allowed to become still. What we may overlook in this example is that in great completion practice we are not watching the water. We are the water. The natural clarity of water often goes unnoticed, unrecognized and unappreciated. Because it is transparent, we do not see it. We see right through it. The natural clarity of mind is similar. No one has seen it, not even a buddha, and most of us do not recognize or appreciate it.

Mind is not a thing we watch. If we are watching mind, we are already one step removed. If we are trying to change what we our experiencing, or trying to analyze or track it, we are more than one step removed. Every movement — whether it is checking our experience, managing it or anticipating it (goal-seeking) — stirs up the water that is our mind, along with all the sediment. The empty clarity is there, but we will not know it as long as we keep stirring things up.

Mind is also likened to a mirror. We never see a mirror. We know a mirror is there only because we see reflections in the mirror. The natural clarity of the mirror itself is transparent. In the same way, we easily miss this subtle clear awareness. We do not see it. We see right through it.

By now I know that checking my experience, or tracking or analyzing it, is pointless. No matter what logic scheme I may appeal to — psychology, sociology, neurology, biology, or astrology, to name only a few — none of them can tell me what my life is. Those perspectives may be helpful for problems in other contexts, but for the direct awareness that Jigmé Lingpa is talking about, they are worse than useless. They rely on concepts, ideas about life. I still check my experience while I am meditating, asking myself "How am I doing?" Sometimes I fall into tracking a thought and how one thought leads to another or analyzing what I am experiencing. The difference is that now, as soon as I notice what am I doing, I move from the tracking or the analyzing back into whatever I am experiencing right now.

There are two points here. First, I had to reach the place where I knew that these approaches were fruitless. Second, even with that knowledge, I still have to cut the pattern of checking, again and again. I am practicing being in what arises in experience, without trying to change it. On the one hand, this new way is the epitome of natural in that it just lets experience be what it is. On the other, at least in the beginning, it is not at all natural. *No judgment, no appraisal, no story* is a way of relating to what arises that we are not used to and not practiced in.

The same holds for managing my experience, the persistent and pernicious tendency to want things to be just a little different from what they are. In meditation, I find myself tweaking this here, adjusting that there, and before I know it, I am quite involved in trying to make my experience conform to my expectations. Again, the same principle holds. As soon as I recognize what I am doing, I return to whatever I am experiencing right then.

In some ways I find goal-seeking the hardest. One would think that with all the disappointments and defeats, I would no longer pay attention to small victories in the quality of attention. Nevertheless, when my mind becomes very quiet or very clear, when there is a sense of infinite space or profound depth, a thought will often pop up, "Ah, now I am getting somewhere." When that happens, there is a rueful smile of recognition, and I open to that and rest right there.

Verse 3.9

Then, when conceptual thinking arises,
Don't look at what arises: be what knows the arising.
Like an oak peg in hard ground,
Stand firm in awareness that knows,
And go deep into the mystery.

What do you do when a thought arises? This is a central question in virtually every contemplative tradition.

As I noted in the introduction to this section, this verse exhibits the genius of the Tibetan tradition of Buddhism. In just four lines in the Tibetan, Jigmé Lingpa gives precise instruction on one of the deepest aspects of meditation practice, connects it with the tradition of radical dzogchen that he initiated — the teachings of the *Heart Drop Cycle* — differentiates the *Heart Drop* approach from other approaches, and provides a vivid simile for practice.

When we have no training or insight, we take our thoughts as having meaning and needing to be acted on. If they are not given expression, then they have to be restrained or even suppressed.

Soon after we begin meditation practice, we see that, in the words of Henepola Gunaratana, our minds are shrieking, gibbering madhouses, completely out of our control. As we progress in practice, we see more and more that the problem is not in what thoughts we experience but how we experience them. We discover new possibilities, a clear open awareness in which thoughts, feelings and sensations simply come and go. We sense the possibility of being free — free from having to react, free of habituated patterns of behavior and free of naïve ideas about how things are.

Different practice traditions take different approaches to the arising of thoughts. Most esoteric traditions agree that thoughts themselves are not the enemy. On the other hand, when we are thinking, awareness is dulled and confused. Some traditions encourage the development of a dispassionate observer, but that simply replaces one problem with another. The direct-awareness traditions of Tibet teach the possibility of an awareness in which there is no observer; an awareness in which thoughts, feelings and sensations form and dissolve like mist or like clouds in the sky.

Yet, when thoughts do arise, it is all too easy to fall out of such clear open awareness into dull confused thinking. The usual approach found in the middle way, mahamudra, dzogchen and chö teachings is to look right at thought as it arises. In *A Summary of the Key Points in Creation and Completion*, Kongtrul points out that the instruction for mahamudra and dzogchen is usually given this way:

> Whatever thought arises, when you look right at it
> And do nothing with it, it releases and you ride the shift.

Here, Jigmé Lingpa is presenting a different approach. When a thought arises, do not look at the thought. Instead, *be what knows the arising*. Kongtrul later says much the same thing in these words:

> Whatever arises, look inward, right at what knows the thought.

What happens when you do this? You end up looking at nothing and, simultaneously, being nothing. Any vestige of an observer evaporates, and along with it, any engagement with conceptual thinking. If your attention is sufficiently stable (and that is the challenge for most people in this practice), you are standing in awareness. Then, as Jigmé Lingpa writes, you stand like an oak peg in hard ground—you are there and you do not move. The awareness takes you where it takes you, deep into the mystery.

What is this mystery? The mystery is nothing—nothing whatsoever. As Gertrude Stein said of Oakland, California, "There is no there there." People talk endlessly about this nothing. It has been given many names, but that is itself a problem. It has been called emptiness, buddha nature, pure being or experience itself (Skt. *dharmatā*), basic space of experience (Skt. *dharmadhatu*), and so on. The philosophers make precise distinctions between all these terms, buttressing their distinctions with rigorous definitions. Frequently, they forget that they are talking about an experience or a range of experiences. For those who encounter them, these experiences are so powerful, so meaningful, so wonderful and so transformative that they feel the experiences must reflect a deeper reality, in some sense of that strange and mysterious word. The language of poetry—the language of metaphor, allusion and awe—then gives way to the language of philosophy—definition, distinctions and reason. Reification takes place. An experience becomes a memory and then an idea. Unnoticed, it becomes a belief and then an ideology. The sad result of this process is that people end up fighting wars on the basis of their ideologies, when, in fact, they have just had different experiences.

When we look at what knows, we enter a mystery. We go into the mystery as far as we want or are able to go. It will probably change our lives. Even so, there is no need to make the mystery into anything else. It is how we experience life—nothing more.

Verse 3.10

> Even in this experience of naked presence
> In which there is no movement or change,
> If you don't avoid the mire of position-based correctives,
> You lose your way in analysis and speculation.

At the 2003 retreat at Tara Mandala, every day I walked down the hill from my cabin to the dining area and up the hill to the main house where we met for teaching and group meditation. Up and down, up and down, several times a day — it was good exercise. One day while I was walking down the hill, I saw the grass bending in front of me as the wind swept over it, but it seemed as though nothing was moving. I saw the branches of trees swaying in the wind, but nothing was moving. It was as if the ground had dropped out of something in me and I was looking into a bottomless space in which there was absolutely no movement — not inside, not outside, not anywhere. I had heard and read the Tibetan phrase *po-gyur mé-pa* (Tib. *'pho 'gyur med pa*), literally *no movement or change*, and had often wondered what it referred to. Now the meaning was vividly clear. It meant just that — no movement, no change, even as there was obviously movement and change. How strange! How wonderful!

We read these phrases, or we hear them, and we may think we understand them, but it is quite a different matter when those experiences arise. Words that seemed paradoxical and puzzling make complete sense even though they defy logic and reason. In direct-awareness practice, there are many words and phrases whose meanings can only be known experientially — *emptiness*, for example, or *clarity*, or *no base, no root*, to name just a few. The words and phrases that refer to specific kinds of experience are, in fact, very accurate — it is hard to think of a better description.

When we put our experience into words, however, others hear only the words. If they do not know the experience themselves, they do not make the connection between the words and the experience we are describing. They are unable to see the moon to which our finger is pointing. It is as if we are tapping out the rhythm of a melody and expect the person listening to be able to identify the melody.

All these words and phrases point to a groundless knowing, a groundless presence. Because it is difficult for many of us to meet that groundless knowing, let alone live it, we seek explanations and understandings for our lives and the world in which we live. Even when we experience immediate and naked presence, we still seek explanations. Buddhist texts are full of detailed analyses of experience and awareness and compelling explanations of why things are the way they are. These explanations are all conceptual. While they were usually developed to remedy mistakes in practice or understanding, many practitioners hold on to them as representing some kind of truth. Over time the explanations solidify into beliefs and positions. Practitioners become mired in study, debate, analysis and speculation — sometimes for generations. Many of those explanations, however, are just the dust left behind by extraordinary practitioners who have lost their way.

Great completion practice is not about philosophy. It is not about truth or reality. It is about being awake and present in this experience we call life, in what we are experiencing right now. As soon as we take a position and say, "This is how things are," we have stepped out of the present moment and back into a world of analysis and speculation. Life is a mystery. Experience is a mystery. Awareness is a mystery. A mystery can be known, it can be experienced, but it cannot be put into words.

Verse 3.11

> All the conventions of outlook, practice and behavior
> Are, in terms of what is natural, just intellectual chaff.
> Let correctives aimed at attention subside into space.
> With the chosen discipline of not being concerned about wandering,
> Just let things be — don't change anything at all.
> In a space beyond all complications and effort
> Lies a great treasure — no thought, no thinking.

Recall the story that Jigmé Lingpa alluded to at the beginning of this poem. A poor man travels far and wide, searching the world for a secret treasure. He fails to find it, no matter where he goes, no matter whom he seeks for advice. The last sage he can find tells him to tend to a tree growing in the garden behind his own house. With nowhere else to go, no one else to see, he returns home and finds that the tree is dying. Something is wrong with its roots. Digging in the soil, he uncovers a chest full of gold. His search is over. What he was seeking was in his own garden all along.

The story is helpful because it reminds us that what we seek, whether we call it freedom, enlightenment, buddha nature, direct awareness, God or The Great Other, is not "out there." It is a little confounding, too, because, even when we feel we understand the story, it is not clear how to do what it is telling us to do. I could not find the tree, let alone the chest of gold, because I did not know where to look.

Mind is a mystery. It includes how we experience life, how we experience ourselves and how we experience the world. In this sense, there is nothing in our experience that is not mind.

As meditation practice deepens, we become less and less concerned with the *what* of experience and more and more concerned with the *how*. This shift is not without its challenges. Because of our physical, emotional and cognitive conditioning, what we experience triggers, provokes or kindles a wide range of somatic, emotional and cognitive reactions. For those of us who are drawn or compelled to pursue direct awareness, all those reactions are just stuff, and we build an increasing capacity to experience them as movement rather than fact. In the process, we discover a kind of awareness that is just there, clear and immediate. Sometimes we happen on it by accident, sometimes it is pointed out to us and sometimes it becomes evident to us only after years of effort. No matter how we come to it, once we know it and see its implications, life is never the same. We know what it is to be confused and we know what it is to be clear.

Now we enter a deep and difficult paradox. On the one hand, ideas, explanations, frameworks, techniques and guidelines have little relevance. If we hold on to any of these, we fall back into the confusion of ordinary conceptual knowing. On the other hand, conversations still take place, food is eaten and the tasks of the day are done. It is as if life takes place in the awareness — but whose life? It is not clear. As a separate entity, *I* cease to be part of the picture.

Depending on our training, we may have developed certain abilities that have become second nature to us. In creation-phase practice, for instance, we expand the power and scope of attention by sending out light, deities, dakinis or messengers to every corner of the universe and then drawing in the vitality and energy of the universe to the core of our being. In completion-phase practice, we similarly train in generating, guiding and spreading energy and in dissolving all conceptual experience. Through other practices, we become adept at detecting and correcting imbalances in order to nurture clear stable attention. Practitioners in some traditions train to be acutely aware of wandering and not wandering or to be aware of subtle differences in physical sensations in the body. Naturally, the patterns formed through our training are also going to arise when we sit and rest. If we try to block them or stop them, we create imbalances.

Jigmé Lingpa's instruction is that as these habits of practice arise, we still do nothing. We do not do anything to change or alter our experience. We rest in direct immediate awareness, letting even the habits of practice arise and subside. Strangely, this both deepens the experience of these practices and releases our investment in them. Again, this is not the same as observing them, which involves taking a stance that is somewhat separate from experience.

Sometimes it is like being aware while being inside the practice. Sometimes it seems that practice takes place inside the awareness. A common metaphor for mind and awareness is the ocean. We are in the water, we are the water, but we are not just the waves at the surface. Nor are we just the still depths. We are all of it, and we are all of it without thinking that we are all of it. As soon as we think we are all of it, we are back into conceptual experience.

The last line of this verse, *a great treasure — no thought, no thinking,* brings us back to the theme of the treasure. This line, like many others, is susceptible to misinterpretation. It is not that all thought or thinking ceases or, in terms of the sky metaphor, that there are never any clouds in the sky. Clouds form and dissolve, but the sky does not obstruct them. They come and go on their own. Likewise, neither floating white clouds nor heavy dark thunderheads obstruct the expanse of the sky. The sky, with or without clouds, is still the sky.

When we can be both the sky and the clouds or the water and the waves, then, when we are in great physical or emotional pain, when our world is a complete mess and we do not know what to do, when nothing makes any sense and we do not know where to turn — even then — we are no longer lost in misery and confusion. Like the sky, we can still open to it all and be at peace, and that is the great treasure.

Many of us, it seems, have to take the journey, work through many challenges and endure many hardships before we truly give up, return home and rest — only to discover what has been there all along.

Verse 3.12

> To know that from the beginning there is no awakening
> Is to be where wanting has never been.
> With this special teaching that rots the roots of samsara,
> Wake up from the realm of misery.

Experience arises. Because of our conditioning, we want what we experience to be a little different from what it is — almost all of the time. We constantly push away what we do not like, cling to what we do like and ignore what we do not care about. Each of those reactions involves an effort.

When we discover the possibility of making no effort — no effort whatsoever — the whole edifice of ordinary experience crumbles. It crumbles because ordinary experience rests on the three fundamental emotional reactions: attraction, aversion and indifference.

Buddha? Full awakening? What is that? We discover that we were never asleep to begin with, even though it feels as if we have woken up from a dream.

Wanting? What is that? Where there is nothing to grasp or oppose, wanting does not even enter the picture.

In other words, samsara has come to an end.

What is this *special teaching*? When the Sixteenth Karmapa, Rangjung Rigpé Dorjé, visited us in the three-year retreat, this is what he taught:

"Look," he said, and he stared straight into I know not what, his eyes wide open, almost bulging, as the air in the room crackled with energy.

"As soon as a thought arises, rest," he said as he relaxed his posture, and a wave of warm energy flooded the room.

"Then look again," he said, and again it felt as if the air was made of lightning.

"Do you see?" he demanded, and then he would do it again.

His teaching had all the subtlety of someone picking me up by the scruff of my neck and throwing me against a wall — over and over. I do not remember how many times. I just remember being repeatedly thrown against a wall.

"This is what I've understood from my study and practice in Mahamudra, Dzogchen and Kalachakra," he concluded, and then he left.

As I worked with this alternation over many years, the looking and the resting gradually came together, and practice required less and less exertion. It seemed that there was nothing to do, and this not-doing culminated unexpectedly in a sudden shattering understanding that there was absolutely nothing to oppose. With nothing to oppose, there was nothing about which I could say, "I am not that." A whole way of defining who I am crumbled. The very basis for reaction, the need to reshape what arises in experience, crumbled, too. All the usual reference points — up, down, forward, backward, good, bad — were gone. I could just let things be in a peace, or a freedom, that was quite different from anything I had experienced before. And it was always there.

I continued (and continue) to sit regularly, but any notion of practice as such has gone. At the same time, this understanding has brought me closer to the feeling that I am actually in my life, and that is a tangible freedom. While my life has been shaped by many influences — my genetic inheritance, my parents and family, school and education, friends and colleagues, my training in Buddhism, the teachers and students I have worked with, the three-year retreats, as well as work, health and the societies and cultures in which I have lived — my life is just life. It does not belong to anyone or anything, not even to me.

Verse 3.13

When you open and relax,
There is an emptiness that goes beyond true or false.
Here, if you know arising release, natural release and direct release,
You are no different from all the awakened ones.
You are awake and no different from me.

It sounds so simple. Just open and relax. But the opening and relaxing to which Jigmé Lingpa refers is not quite what we do when we come home from work and let the cares of the day subside. Nor is it what we do when we go on a vacation. He is talking about the opening and relaxing that takes place when we cease to do anything, when we let go of any effort whatsoever. This is not easy. Our whole being is keyed to striving. Biologically we strive to stay alive. Emotionally we strive for connection and fulfillment. Cognitively we strive to construct and maintain a consistent narrative of the "I" that we think we are.

Letting go is not simply an act of will. It happens, although more often by accident than by design. However, as Chögyam Trungpa once said, the purpose of practice is to make ourselves accident-prone.

People have described that letting go in different ways: we become an empty mirror; mind and body drop away; we fall into an emptiness that goes beyond true or false; and many more. Then others seize on our words and miss what we are saying.

Emptiness is not a thing. At the same time it is not nothing. It is a description of an experience, or, possibly, a way of experiencing. It is not a statement about the ground of being or anything like that.

What is that way of experiencing? Here, ordinary language fails because it relies on and generates conceptual thinking. We can use only the language of metaphor, and there are several to choose from — a young child in a cathedral, snowflakes on a hot stone, a knotted snake, or a thief entering an empty house. Jigmé Lingpa is referring to these metaphors in the third line of this verse:

Here, if you know arising release, natural release, and direct release...

Arising release refers to the way experience releases itself as it arises.

The first time I saw the Yosemite Valley, my mind just stopped. Sheer cliffs soaring thousands of feet and towering over the tranquil meadows, rivers and lakes of the valley floor — a natural cathedral of incredible grandeur.

When we look at mind, when we look at nothing and actually see nothing, something similar happens. All the usual busyness disappears and the mind stops. It is not something we make happen, but it happens. This is not just the quiet mind. It is no mind (not literally, of course, but that is how the experience arises). No thinking, no conceptualization, no good, bad, true or false — nothing.

Sometimes, too, when thoughts arise, they vanish in the moment of arising, like snowflakes landing on a hot stone. These beautiful intricate structures, in incomprehensible numbers, swirl, dance and — one by one — vanish in an instant, without trace. Thoughts can be experienced the same way.

Natural release refers to a slightly different experience, the way knots formed in thinking untie themselves. It is as if we are inside a thought as it arises, and like a knotted snake, it unties itself. The thought is gone and we are left in empty space, somewhere over the Grand Canyon or in the Hubble Gap — again, not because of any effort we make. The thought just unties itself.

In *direct release*, there is nothing for a thought to attach to. Like a thief in an empty house, a thought arises, wanders around for a while and then goes. There is no confusion, because there is nothing to be confused. Perhaps a whole gang of thoughts comes barging in. Still, there is nothing for them to connect to, nothing they can take or push against or steal. At some point they just leave.

In all of this, the "I" plays no role. "I" is based in thought, in language, but here there are no words. I do not release thoughts. Thoughts release themselves. All the other qualities of awakening follow from that.

As thoughts release themselves, the groundlessness of all experience is revealed to us over and over again. The nature of that groundlessness is a clarity that frees us from confused notions about how things are and from the compulsion to react. Everything we say and do from that groundlessness is an expression of compassion, where compassion is not an emotion as such, but simply the way empty clarity responds to what arises.

Verse 3.14

> In this age of strife, these vital instructions for the great mysteries
> Are mingled with the canonical writings of the analytic approach.
> A knowledge-holder who is not different from me
> Will make my revelations clear.
>
> Embodiments of the awakening beings of the three families, masters of this teaching,
> And those blessed with natural talent, enjoy and make use of it.

The phrase *this age of strife* appears frequently in traditional religions. It expresses a worldview shared by many traditional societies and traditional religions. In their mythic cosmologies, as one goes back in time, teachers and rulers are increasingly regarded as noble, wise and virtuous. Consequently, one looks to the past for examples of perfection in human behavior. Likewise, as one moves forward in time, the more corrupt, debased and problematic the world and its rulers become. The cosmology of traditional Buddhism is based on a similar myth of progressive devolution of human behavior and society—from a mythical golden age to the dark and troubled times of the present. In contrast, many modern schools of thought, though they carefully avoid the label *religious*, are based on the equally questionable myth of progressive evolution to an ideal society brought about by a higher consciousness or a technological utopia.

However, what Jigmé Lingpa says next is important:

> ... these vital instructions for the great mysteries
> Are mingled with the canonical writings of the analytic approach.

In earlier verses, Jigmé Lingpa has been clear that the analytic approach is different from direct-awareness teachings such as great completion. The relationship between the two is analogous to the relationship between the theory of music and instructions in how to play a musical instrument. Because the analytic approach is based in concept and language, it cannot bring us into the direct experience of, say, the various kinds of releasing described in the preceding verse any more than a description of the principles of composition can enable us to play a piece of music.

Jigmé Lingpa was self-taught and thus less invested in the analytic approach than his academically trained colleagues. The words he puts into the mouth of Ever-present Good are very clear in their meaning: rely on a teacher who knows awareness experientially to differentiate between direct-awareness practice and practice based on analytical philosophy. The Tibetan in this verse is ambiguous, however, and could be interpreted as a prophecy, foretelling the coming of such a teacher. It could be a reference to Jigmé Lingpa himself.

The guidance Jigmé Lingpa offers in this poem is not for beginners. Milarepa started with a similar practice — *buddhahood without meditation*. He took the instruction "Do nothing" literally. He did not do anything. He just sat around, eating and sleeping. Fortunately, his dzogchen teacher saw that this practice was not going to work for Milarepa and directed him to Marpa. Under Marpa's guidance, Milarepa developed the understanding, skills and abilities he needed to practice. In the same way, most of us, if we practice this way without preparation, will end up doing nothing and going nowhere, but in the wrong way. This is why, in traditional contexts, texts such as this one were sealed — to be shown and taught only to those who could benefit from them.

In the last two lines, Jigmé Lingpa says explicitly that he is not writing for everyone, but for those who have already mastered such practice and for those who have natural talent. A few talented people will be able to make immediate use of the instruction Jigmé Lingpa offers here. For most of us, though, the subtlety and depth of these teachings reveal themselves only as our understanding and abilities develop. It is through the unfolding of our own experience that we are able to enjoy and engage them as Jigmé Lingpa intended.

Acknowledgments

A book goes through many stages, from its inception to the final manuscript, from the manuscript to its publication and from its publication to the hands of the reader. My thanks and appreciation to the many people who provided support and advice at each of these stages.

First and foremost, I am grateful to Kilung Rinpoche. This book would never have been conceived if he had not entrusted me with the translation of Jigmé Lingpa's poem. Ingrid McLeod provided invaluable assistance, and the translation that appears here has been much improved by her suggestions.

As for the commentary, Ruth Gilbert and Jon Parmenter kindly took the time to offer helpful comments and suggestions on two successive versions. Again Ingrid, along with Anne Klein, Charles Goodman, Ulrich Kuestner, Donna McLaughlin and Shawn Woodyard also pointed out a number of areas where the text could be improved.

Once a manuscript is complete, it still needs to be corrected, and for this task, I am grateful to Christy Stebbins for her painstaking efforts.

Valerie Brewster designed both the book and the cover. Ann Braun found the cover photo, and Kaz Ogino suggested the title. Diana Chang took the photo in the Namib Desert and kindly gave me permission to use it for the cover.

After a book is published, it still has to be made known to the world, and I am grateful to Juliana Balistreri, Judy Herzl and Ellen Kleiner for their advice, help and efforts in this regard. For the promotional videos, my thanks to Odin Halverson and Lynea Diaz-Hagen as well as Dan Pappalardo, Dale Everett, Jake Braasladt and everyone at Troika Design Group. Deborah Neikirk and Art Gardner also helped prepare publicity materials, both print and digital.

Finally, my thanks to those who have studied with me and who make use of the resources available on Unfettered Mind's website. This book is very much the result of your curiousity, support and encouragement.

Bibliography

Bibliographic references in order of appearance

page 3   chos-dbyings rin-po-che'i mdzod, kLong-chen-pa Dri-me-'od-zer
English translations: *The Precious Treasury of the Basic Space of Phenomena*, translated by Richard Barron. *Spaciousness: The Radical Dzogchen of the Vajra-Heart: Longchenpa's Treasury of the Dharmadhatu*, translated by Keith Dowman

page 4   *Reflections on Silver River*, Ken McLeod

page 4   *Essays in Zen Buddhism*, D. T. Suzuki

page 4   *The Wisdom of the Desert*, Thomas Merton

page 5   Collected Letters, Albert Einstein

page 6   *Cloud of Unknowing*, anonymous

page 6   *Debt: The First 5000 Years*, David Graeber

page 7   *Seven Treasuries* (Tib. mdzod bdun), kLong-chen-pa Dri-me-'od-zer

page 7   *Heart Drop Cycle* (Tib. klong-chen snying-thig), 'Jig-med gLing-pa

page 9   tshig gsum gnad brdeg attributed to Garab Dorje

page 44   *F.O.A. — Full on Arrival*, anonymous

page 64   *An Essay on Man*, Alexander Pope

page 65   *Through the Looking-Glass, and What Alice Found There*, Lewis Carroll

page 65   *Four Quartets*, T. S. Eliot

page 67   *Tao Te Ching*, Lao Tzu

page 68   *Everything Yearned For*, Manhae, translated by Francisca Cho

page 68   *Mind Training in Eight Verses* (Tib. blo sbyong tshigs rkang brgyad ma), dGe-bshes Glang-ri Thang-pa (pron. Lang-ri Tang-pa), translated by Ken McLeod

page 70   *Letters to a Young Poet*, Rainer Maria Rilke, translated by M.D. Herter Norton

page 71   *The Divine Comedy*, Dante Alighieri

page 72   *The Book of the Book*, Idries Shah

page 72   *The Great Path of Awakening*, Jamgön Kongtrul, translated by Ken McLeod

page 73   *The Secret Pilgrim*, John Le Carré

page 77   *The Gateless Gate*, Wumen Huikai

page 80   *A Summary of the Key Points in Creation and Completion* (Tib. lam-zhugs-kyi-gang-zag las-dang-po-pa la phan-pa'i bskyed rdzogs kyi gnad bsdus), Jamgön Kongtrul
English translation: *Creation and Completion*, translated by Sarah Harding

page 90   *The Gateless Gate*, Wumen Huikai
page 93   *Tao Te Ching*, Lao Tzu, translation by Ken McLeod
page 100 *A Light in the Dark*, Ju Mipam Jampal Dorjé, translated by Ken McLeod
page 111 *Mindfulness in Plain English*, Bhante Henepola Gunaratana

About the Author

Ken Mcleod is known for his ability to explain deep and subtle teachings in clear and simple language. "He distills the nature and purpose of Buddhism to make it accessible for any newcomer without dumbing it down," writes Phil Catalfo (*Yoga Journal*, July 2001) in his review of Ken's first book *Wake Up to Your Life*.

Born in England in 1948, Ken grew up in Canada and journeyed overland to India (in large part by bicycle) in 1969–70. There he met his principal teacher, Kalu Rinpoche. Ken served as his interpreter in India as well as during Kalu Rinpoche's first two teaching tours in North America. After Ken completed two three-year retreats, he was appointed to teach in Los Angeles. In 1990, Ken established Unfettered Mind, a place for people whose paths lie outside established centers and institutions.

In 1996, Ken roiled the Buddhist world with his model of one-on-one consultations on Buddhist practice. His approach is now regarded as a viable model for Buddhist teachers in the West. In addition to retreats and courses, Ken also conducted teacher training programs and mentored a number of newer teachers. He continues to do so on an informal basis.

In 1999, Ken established a consulting practice focusing on leadership skills, team building and personal and organizational effectiveness.

Ken has a graduate degree in mathematics from the University of British Columbia (Canada), more than twenty years intensive training in Eastern disciplines (including Buddhism, tai chi and other martial arts), and over thirty years teaching and consulting experience.